CAP-BADGES
OF THE
BRITISH ARMY
1939–45

CAP-BADGES
OF THE
BRITISH ARMY
1939–45

G.L.D. ALDERSON

First published 2007
This edition published 2014
by Spellmount, an imprint of

The History Press
The Mill, Brimscombe Port
Stroud, Gloucestershire, GL5 2QG
www.thehistorypress.co.uk

British Library Cataloguing in Publication Data.
A catalogue record for this book is available from the British Library.

ISBN 978 0 7524 9969 7

Typesetting and origination by The History Press
Printed in Great Britain

Contents

Foreword

As memories of the Second World War become more and more clouded with the passing of time, it is becoming increasingly difficult to separate fact from fiction in men's minds. The conflicting accounts of the major campaigns by those participating are perhaps the prime example of the difficulties one faces in attempting to determine what actually happened.

However, the paradox which exists is that as the memories become more ill-defined, there is an increasing interest in the Second World War. What is true on the great scale of strategies of armies, is no less true at the level of minutiae of equipment and insignia. Nowhere is this interest shown more than in that facet of military history which concentrates on the cap-badges of the British Army.

Unlike their United States and Continental counterparts, the regiments of the British Army have always set great store by their cap-badges which, in miniature, encapsulated the history and traditions of the units which wore them. This was particularly so among the infantry which is perhaps surprising, insofar as many of the regiments in the Second World War were of quite recent origin – historically speaking. The cap-badges, which were worn through the two world wars by the County Regiments which formed the bulk of the infantry, date no further back than the late nineteenth century, following the Cardwell reforms.

While of relatively recent origin, the cap-badge absorbed a far older territorial loyalty, which can almost be traced back to the tribal loyalty in the ages before the Norman Conquest and which has been reinforced down the ages. For example, although the Wars of the Roses were dynastic, not territorial, in origin one can see how the competition between those on the East and West of the Pennines has developed a man's loyalty to a particular colour of rose. Other counties have similar rallying symbols and the County Regiments were themselves expressions of pride just as surely as those symbols.

With changes in military warfare presaged towards the end of the Second World War and the need for fewer infantrymen, the need for the County Regiments disappeared and most were absorbed into the much larger regiments of the '60s and '70s. As a result very few regiments retain the identity which they nurtured through two world wars. In many cases, the amalgamations were accepted with more or less good grace, while others were hatchet jobs initiated by bureaucrats with no thought for local feelings.

If the reduction of the Infantry of the Line has been dramatic, even that has been overshadowed, in terms of reduction of regiments, by the total disappearance of the county yeomanry regiments. True, at the time of writing, four yeomanry regiments exist in various guises, but these four represent all that remain after several successive amalgamations and none has any attachment to a particular county. Because the majority of yeomanry regiments had no permanent cadre of long-serving Regular personnel, there are few records of their war-time experiences – a situation which was further complicated by the increased demand for artillery regiments in the Second World War.

As a result of this demand, many yeomanry regiments were forced to abandon their cavalry role and become part of the Royal Regiment of Artillery. Whether these regiments retained their cap-badges or adopted that of their new parent regiment seems often to have depended upon local circumstances and personalities. Certainly there were no hard and fast rules on what badges were worn. Any attempt to ascertain which badges were worn during the Second World War by these erstwhile artillery regiments was further complicated by the fact that, shortly after the end of hostilities, a number of yeomanry regiments were transferred to the Royal Armoured Corps and immediately resumed their former badges. Some fifty years on, it is becomingly increasingly difficult to isolate those badges which were worn in the relatively short period – in historical terms – which this book seeks to cover.

All the photographs have been taken from my own collection of badges, but I have catalogued and described only those badges worn by Other Ranks. For that reason, neither of the badges worn by the Royal Army Chaplains' Department have been listed. Furthermore, I have not attempted to describe or list the badges of the various special forces raised in the 1939–45 War. I have excluded them for two reasons: first, most of them are outside the budget of the average collector and, secondly, most of the badges which are available on the market are of doubtful provenance.

Originally, the information in this second edition appeared in two separate volumes but those who bought the first almost invariably bought the second. As there was a need for some slight amendments to the text and a requirement to add four regiments which had escaped my initial investigations, I was advised to combine the two volumes in the belief that a single book would be more convenient for the collector. I have, however, maintained the previous format, so that units generally appear under the arm of the service to which they were allotted at the beginning of the war.

In the interests of convenience I have taken one or two liberties with this overall scheme. For example, although the Lovat Scouts were officially classified in the Army List as Scouts, they were employed as infantry from early 1940 and, therefore, appear as such in Section VII. Similarly, for ease of identification, I have listed the five Territorial battalions who continued to wear their own cap-badges while serving with the Royal Artillery, under their infantry titles, even though all five had transferred to the Royal Engineers as searchlight regiments in 1938 before moving to the artillery in 1940.

For the yeomanry regiments and Territorial battalions which converted to artillery, but continued to wear their own badges, I have also added the subsequent titles by which they were known.

In addition, I have added details of the backing or the inserts worn behind many of the cap-badges. Although some regiments, like the majority of Scottish formations, had always worn a backing to their badges, many others adopted a badge backing only after the introduction of the cap GS. Almost invariably, the patches which were adopted were drawn from the regimental colours of the regiments' antecedents; for example, the Essex Regiment adopted a patch of 'Pompadour' purple of the 56th Foot, while the Middlesex adopted a bi-coloured patch which invoked the colours of the two regiments from which it had been formed in 1881. Others, like the Inniskilling Fusiliers, drew on more recent history for the backing to their badges. Whatever the origins, the backings gave a splash of colour to the cap GS, surely the nadir of military headwear.

In conclusion, I hope that the information in the following pages will enable those wishing to complete a collection of Second World War cap-badges of the British Army to do so in the knowledge that those illustrated and described were indeed issued and worn by the formations shown during that period.

The interest for me in compiling this book has been in removing the layers of time and, in some instances, confusion which surrounded the wearing or otherwise of cap-badges by British Army formations during the Second World War. This interest was enhanced by the generous co-operation which I received from a whole range of people: from curators of museums and those occupying honorary positions in regimental associations, to old soldiers with pride in their regiments. Without this advice and assistance, much of what I have compiled would have had to remain hidden.

Acknowledgements

I should like to thank all those who assisted me by offering advice and information on a number of the badges whose descriptions were either flawed or incomplete when they appeared in the first edition of this book; their contributions were most welcome.

The photographs in this edition have again been taken by my old friend, Gwilym Rees, whose patience and expertise are reflected throughout this book. The photograph on the front of the jacket is of the Gordon Highlanders embarking at the East India Docks for Normandy, see page 206 (courtesy Imperial War Museum, ref. B5216).

Finally, I should like to place on record my thanks to Mrs Beverley Hogg, without whose invaluable advice and assistance this book would never have appeared.

SECTION I

THE HOUSEHOLD CAVALRY

THE LIFE GUARDS

The Royal Cypher of King George VI, pierced within a circlet inscribed 'THE LIFE GUARDS', the whole surmounted by an Imperial Crown. The badge is in bronze.

The Life Guards is the senior, although not the oldest, regiment in the British Army. The origins of the regiment date back to the exile of Charles II during the Commonwealth when a number of Royalists formed a bodyguard for the future king. At the Restoration they were incorporated into the army troops of Horse Guards. In 1788, following a major restructuring of the army, these troops were formed into the 1st and 2nd Regiments of Life Guards.

However, the two regiments were amalgamated in 1922, and it was then that the above cap-badge was introduced.

During the Second World War, The Life Guards, together with The Royal Horse Guards, formed two active service regiments: 1st and 2nd Household Cavalry Regiments. Personnel from The Life Guards and The Royal Horse Guards served together in both these units, but continued to wear their own cap-badges.

THE ROYAL HORSE GUARDS (THE BLUES)

The Royal Cypher of King George VI, pierced, within a circlet inscribed 'ROYAL HORSE GUARDS', the whole being surmounted by an Imperial Crown. The badge is in bronze.

The other regiment in the Household Cavalry, and next to The Life Guards in order of precedence, was The Royal Horse Guards. Unlike The Life Guards, The Royal Horse Guards was descended from the Parliamentary side in the English Civil War. At the Restoration, the regiment was absorbed into the Royalist Army as the Royal Regiment of Horse.

Initially commanded by the Earl of Oxford, whose livery was blue, the regiment adopted a blue uniform on its inception in 1661. Although Lord Oxford ceased to be colonel in 1688, the regiment retained its original blue uniform and thus acquired its unofficial title of 'The Blues'. The regiment underwent several changes of title during the eighteenth century, receiving the above nomenclature in 1819, when 'The Blues' was officially incorporated into its title.

Until this date, The Blues had occupied a unique, though somewhat indefinite, place in the British Army. Although it was a regiment with strong royal connections and was expected to share duties with The Life Guards, its status lay somewhere between that of The Life Guards and the senior regiment of the Cavalry of the Line. In 1820, however, as a compliment to its colonel, the Duke of Wellington, and in consideration of its distinguished service at Waterloo, the regiment was granted the full status of Household Cavalry, until then only enjoyed by The Life Guards.

Joining The Life Guards in the Household Cavalry Regiments, The Royal Horse Guards initially formed part of the 1st Cavalry Division and saw action in the Middle East in 1940. Eventually both regiments were re-equipped with armoured cars, and after service in the Western Desert and Italy, they were transferred to North West Europe.

SECTION II

THE ROYAL ARMOURED CORPS

THE ROYAL ARMOURED CORPS

Two badges were worn:

left. within a laurel wreath, the letters '*RAC*' in script characters. The whole is ensigned with an Imperial Crown. The badge is in gilding metal.

right. a mailed gauntlet for the right hand, fist clenched, palm to the front with a billet on the wrist inscribed '*RAC*'. Issuing from the wrist of the gauntlet, upwards, two concentric circles incomplete, but barbed at the ends. The whole is ensigned with an Imperial Crown which rests on the two uppermost barbs. The badge is in white metal.

Although the Royal Armoured Corps was established in April 1939, the first badge of the corps was not adopted until 1940. This was replaced in 1942 by the second badge – the composition of which represents armour, through the mailed fist, and speed, through the barbed circles.

The Royal Armoured Corps was formed to combine all the British Army's armoured units in the same body and initially it consisted of eighteen mechanised cavalry regiments, eight battalions of the Royal Tank Corps, renamed the Royal Tank Regiment (RTR) on the formation of the Royal Armoured Corps, and eight yeomanry regiments which, until then, had been Territorial armoured car companies of the Royal Tank Corps.

The RAC was originally only responsible for recruiting, and the administration and training of all armoured regiments, with each of the constituent regiments retaining its own identity and its distinctive cap-badge and uniform. It was not until the after the defeat of the BEF in France that the RAC was given greater authority and representation. Six new cavalry regiments were formed under its umbrella between December 1940 and February 1941, while the 1st Royal Dragoons and the Royal Scots Greys became part of the RAC in 1941 and 1942, respectively.

The demand for armoured units continued to grow and a further expansion of the RAC occurred in November 1941 and July 1942 when a number of infantry battalions were converted to numbered RAC regiments. The policy regarding cap-badges of these newly-armoured regiments was far from uniform. While approximately half adopted the black beret and clenched fist badge of the RAC, the remainder merely wore the black beret but retained their infantry badges. The 155th Regiment RAC, which had been the 15th Battalion, The Durham Light Infantry, went one stage further, for while the RAC badge was worn in the beret, the DLI badge continued to be worn in the Field Service Cap!

A list of those RAC regiments which continued to wear their own badges appears at the end of this section.

At its peak strength in late 1942, the RAC comprised 104 active service and 11 training regiments. Of the former, no less than thirty-three were converted infantry battalions and another fifteen were yeomanry battalions which had joined the original eight in the two years following the formation of the Royal Armoured Corps. The number was further augmented in 1944, when the Reconnaissance Corps, comprising no fewer than twenty-six regiments, was transferred to the RAC.

The Royal Armoured Corps fought in all major theatres of war, but perhaps the campaign which most evokes its activities was that in the Western Desert where its units were able to operate without the obstacles encountered in the other areas of operations which extended from North West Europe to Burma.

1ST KING'S DRAGOON GUARDS

The double-headed eagle of the Austrian Empire. The badge is in white metal.

The badge was awarded to the regiment in recognition of the fact that the Emperor of Austria was its Colonel-in-Chief from 1896 until the outbreak of the First World War. Because of Austria's alliance with Germany, the badge was withdrawn in 1915 and from then until 1937 the regiment wore an eight-pointed star surmounted by a crown. However, the eagle was restored on the accession of King George VI.

The senior cavalry regiment of the line, the 1st King's Dragoons, was originally raised by King James II and it was awarded the above title in 1746 when it was converted to Dragoons.

The King's Dragoon Guards was mechanised in 1938 and joined the Royal Armoured Corps as an armoured car unit in which role it initially saw service in the Western Desert.

THE QUEEN'S BAYS (2ND DRAGOON GUARDS)

The word *'BAYS'* in Old English lettering within a wreath of bay leaves and surmounted by an Imperial Crown. The badge is in gilding metal or brass.

The regiment was raised as the 3rd Horse at the time of the rebellion by the Duke of Monmouth in 1685. It underwent several changes of name before becoming the 2nd Dragoon Guards in 1746. The tradition of bay horses dates from the middle of the eighteenth century although the regiment did not receive the above title until 1870.

The title was reinforced in the canting use of bay leaves in the wreath instead of the more usual laurel.

The Queen's Bays was mechanised in 1938 and as a tank regiment first saw active service in the Royal Armoured Corps in the Western Desert.

3RD CARABINIERS
(THE PRINCE OF WALES'S DRAGOON GUARDS)

On a pair of crossed carbines, muzzles uppermost, the Prince of Wales's plumes, coronet and motto. Across the butts of the carbines is a scroll inscribed '*3RD CARABINIERS*'. The coronet and the scroll are in gilding metal and the plumes, the Prince of Wales's motto and the carbines are in white metal.

The 3rd Carabiniers was formed in 1922 from the 3rd Dragoon Guards and the Carabiniers (6th Dragoon Guards). The Prince of Wales's coronet and the plumes on the badge were taken from that of the 3rd Dragoon Guards, while the crossed carbines recall the Carabiniers.

The 3rd Carabiniers was converted to a light tank regiment in 1938 and served throughout the war with the Fourteenth Army in Burma – the only Regular cavalry regiment to do so.

4TH/7TH ROYAL DRAGOON GUARDS

An eight-pointed star thereon a circlet inscribed 'QUIS SEPARABIT – MCMXXII'. Within the circlet, the cross of St George with the coronet of the Princess Royal superimposed. The badge is in white metal.

Badge backing. A maroon square, worn on its point cut to the outer edges of the four main points of the star, was worn behind the badge.

The regiment was formed in 1922 from the 4th Royal Irish Dragoon Guards and the 7th Dragoon Guards (Princess Royal's) and the title 'Royal' was conferred upon it in 1936.

The badge was based on the main devices from the badges of the two constituent regiments which formed the 4th/7th Royal Dragoon Guards. The Star of the Order of St Patrick and the motto 'Quis Separabit' were taken from the 4th Dragoon Guards, while the coronet reflects the secondary title of the 7th Dragoon Guards. The Roman numerals MCMXXII refer to the year in which the regiments were amalgamated.

Converted to armour in 1938, the 4th/7th Royal Dragoon Guards, was the first mechanised cavalry regiment to land in France with the BEF in 1939. It was also the first to return to France on D-Day.

5TH ROYAL INNISKILLING DRAGOON GUARDS

The monogram 'VGD' surmounted by an Imperial Crown. The badge is in white metal.

Badge backing. A red outline to the cap-badge was adopted in 1942.

The 5th Royal Inniskilling Dragoon Guards was the result of another amalgamation which took place in 1922, the two regiments concerned being the 5th Dragoon Guards (Princess Charlotte of Wales's) and the Inniskillings (6th Dragoons). The badge contains no reference to either of these two regiments, basically being a monogram of the new regiment's initials.

The original title of the post-1922 regiment was simply the 5th/6th Dragoon Guards, being altered in 1927 to the 5th Inniskilling Dragoon Guards to clarify the status of the regiment, the original 6th Dragoon Guards having been amalgamated with The Carabiniers. It was granted the tide of 'Royal' in 1935 at the time of the Silver Jubilee of King George V and the above badge dates from then.

The regiment was mechanised in 1938 and joined the Royal Armoured Corps in 1939. It subsequently saw service in North West Europe.

THE ROYAL DRAGOONS

The Royal Crest, a lion on an Imperial Crown, above a scroll inscribed *'THE ROYAL DRAGOONS'*. The Royal Crest is in gilding metal and the scroll in white metal.

The oldest cavalry regiment of the line, The Royal Dragoons was raised in 1661 for the defence of the newly acquired British possession of Tangiers. The Tangier Horse, by which title the regiment was originally known, returned to England in 1764 and was given the title The King's Own Royal Regiment of Dragoons.

The regiment fought at the Battle of Waterloo where it captured the standard of the French 105th Regiment, a representation of which it subsequently took as its cap-badge. However, in 1898, the badge was changed to the Royal Crest. In 1915, the Royal Dragoons reverted to wearing its eagle cap-badge and continued to do so until 1919, when under pressure from the War Office, the Royal Crest was re-instated as the regiment's cap-badge.

The Royal Dragoons was not mechanised until 1940 when it was converted to an armoured car regiment. It saw active service in the Western Desert, Syria and Italy before returning to North West Europe in July 1944.

THE ROYAL SCOTS GREYS (2ND DRAGOONS)

An eagle with a wreath of laurels on its breast upon a plinth inscribed 'WATERLOO'. Below the eagle is a scroll inscribed 'ROYAL SCOTS GREYS'. The eagle is in white metal and the scroll is in gilding metal.

The regiment was established in 1678 when, as the 2nd Dragoons, it was formed from various troops of dragoons in Scotland. Its title was derived from the fact that personnel of the regiment wore grey uniforms and from 1702 they were mounted on grey horses. This name, however, was not officially adopted until 1921, when the present badge was introduced.

The badge was adopted to commemorate the action of Sergeant Ewart of the Royal North British Dragoons (by which title the regiment was known at the time) in capturing the standard of the 45th (Invincibles) Regiment of the French Army at Waterloo in 1815.

The Royal Scots Greys was among the last cavalry regiments to be mechanised, only converting to armour when serving in Palestine in 1941 and not becoming part of the Royal Armoured Corps until 1942. As a tank regiment it saw service in the Western Desert and Sicilian campaigns before returning to the United Kingdom to prepare for the invasion of France in 1944.

3RD THE KING'S OWN HUSSARS

The White Horse of Hanover on ground. Below is a scroll inscribed '*3RD THE KING'S OWN HUSSARS*'. The horse and ground are in white metal and the scroll is in gilding metal.

The 3rd The King's Own Hussars was raised at the time of the Monmouth Rebellion in 1685 when it was known as the Queen Consort's Regiment of Dragoons. Its title was changed to the King's Own Dragoons on the accession of King George I in 1714, and it was from its association with George I that the regiment drew the main device of its badge – that of the White Horse of Hanover. The regiment became hussars in 1861 and the above badge was adopted in 1930 when the scroll was changed to that shown.

In the Second World War, the 3rd The King's Own Hussars saw service with the Desert Rats in the Western Desert and Italian campaigns.

4TH QUEEN'S OWN HUSSARS

A circlet inscribed '*QUEEN'S OWN HUSSARS*' with a spray of laurel in the bottom centre of the circlet. In the centre are the Roman numerals *IV* in ornamental characters. Above the circlet is an Imperial Crown and below it is a scroll inscribed '*MENTE ET MANU*' (with might and main). The numerals and the scroll are in white metal and the remainder of the badge is in gilding metal.

Like the 3rd Hussars, the 4th was another cavalry regiment raised at the time of the Monmouth Rebellion in 1685, its original title being the Princess of Denmark's Regiment of Dragoons. The above title was finally adopted in 1861 when the four remaining regiments of dragoons were converted to hussars. The motto '*Mente et Manu*' had been the regiment's motto since it appeared on a Royal Warrant of 1768. However, the regiment tried unsuccessfully several times to have the motto incorporated onto its badge, but it was not until 1906 that King Edward VII confirmed the regiment's right to do so. Consequently, the badge was altered that year to reflect the king's decision.

The regiment served with the 7th Armoured Division in the Western Desert in 1942 and subsequently fought in the Italian Campaign as part of the Fifth Army.

7TH QUEEN'S OWN HUSSARS

A circlet inscribed '*7TH QUEEN'S OWN HUSSARS*' surmounted by an Imperial Crown. Within the circlet, the monogram '*QO*' is reversed and entwined. The monogram is in white metal and the remainder of the badge is in gilding metal.

The regiment was formed in 1690 from independent troops of cavalry which fought at the Battle of Killiecrankie in 1689. It became the Queen's Regiment of Dragoons in 1729 and was numbered 'the 7th' from 1751. In 1807 it became a hussar regiment and this role and title were reflected in the title on the circlet and in the monogram.

During the Second World War, the 7th Queen's Own Hussars fought in Burma before being transferred to the Italian Campaign.

8TH KING'S ROYAL IRISH HUSSARS

The Irish Harp surmounted by an Imperial Crown. Below the harp is a scroll inscribed '*8TH KING'S ROYAL IRISH HUSSARS*'. The harp is in white metal while the remainder of the badge is in gilding metal.

Raised in Ireland by King William III in 1683, the regiment was numbered 'the 8th' in 1742. It was granted the title of the King's Own Royal Irish Dragoons in 1777 and in 1822 converted to hussars, from which role it took the above title.

The main device of the badge is the Irish Harp which commemorates the geographical origins of the regiment, while the scroll alludes to the regiment's former role as hussars.

The 8th Hussars was one of the first cavalry regiments to be mechanised, serving first with the 7th Armoured Division in the Western Desert and later in North West Europe, where it took part in the drive to Berlin.

9TH QUEEN'S ROYAL LANCERS

On crossed lances, the numeral '9' surmounted by an Imperial Crown. Across the lower ends of the lances and entwining them, a scroll inscribed 'LANCERS'. The badge is in white metal.

The regiment was first raised as dragoons in 1715 to meet the threat of the first Jacobite Rebellion and was subsequently numbered 'the 9th' in 1742. In 1816, it was converted to a regiment of lancers and in 1830 its title was changed in honour of Queen Adelaide, wife of King William IV. The above title was adopted in 1920, but the badge dates from the reign of King Edward VII, being sealed in 1903.

The 9th Queen's Royal Lancers was converted to armour as early as 1935 when it became a light tank regiment, in which role it served with the BEF in France in 1940. In 1941, the regiment was sent to Egypt and subsequently saw service in the Western Desert and Italy.

10TH ROYAL HUSSARS
(PRINCE OF WALES'S OWN)

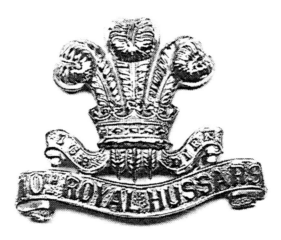

The Prince of Wales's plumes rising from a coronet; the motto '*ICH DIEN*' (I Serve) inscribed on the scrolls on each side of the coronet. Below the coronet; a scroll inscribed '*10TH ROYAL HUSSARS*'. The coronet and scroll are in gilding metal, the remainder is in white metal.

Badge backing. When worn in the cap GS, the badge was backed by a red domed patch.

Raised in 1715, like the 9th Lancers, to meet the threat of the Jacobites, the regiment was originally equipped as dragoons. The then Prince of Wales was appointed Colonel of the Regiment in 1796 which accounts for the main device on the badge. In 1806, the Prince of Wales clothed and equipped the regiment as hussars – thus making it the first hussar regiment in the British Army. The scroll below the coronet records this role.

Like the 9th Lancers, the 10th Royal Hussars saw active service with the BEF in France before being transferred to the Eighth Army in which it fought in the Western Desert and Italy.

11TH ROYAL HUSSARS
(PRINCE ALBERT'S OWN)

The Crest of the Prince Consort, Prince Albert of Saxe-Coburg-Gotha, with a scroll below inscribed with his motto *'TREU UND FEST'* (True and Firm). The badge is in gilding metal.

Raised in 1715 as Honeywood's Dragoons to help maintain the Hanoverian Monarchy against a possible restoration of the Stuarts, the regiment was converted to hussars in 1840. In the same year it provided the escort for Prince Albert on his arrival in England for his marriage to Queen Victoria. In commemoration of this service, the regiment was given the secondary title of 'Prince Albert's Own' and the current badge, sealed in 1894, is based upon his crest. The above title was finally adopted in 1920, but the regiment was probably as well-known by its nick-name, the Cherry Pickers, as it was by its official title.

Of all the units in the Royal Armoured Corps, the 11th Royal Hussars was the only one not required to wear the corps' black beret. Instead, it was allowed to continue to wear its original brown beret. Furthermore, when the latter head-dress was worn, it was worn without any badge.

The 11th Royal Hussars was one of the first two cavalry regiments to be mechanised, being converted to armour in 1928. In the Second World War, after service with the 7th Armoured Division in the Western Desert and Italy, the regiment was transferred to North West Europe, where it was the first British armoured unit to enter Berlin.

12TH ROYAL LANCERS
(PRINCE OF WALES'S)

On a pair of crossed lances with pennons flying outwards, the Prince of Wales's plumes, coronet and motto. Above the plumes and within the heads of the lances, an Imperial Crown. Below the motto and coronet, the Roman numerals 'XII'. The plumes, motto and lower half of the pennons are in white metal and the remainder of the badge is in gilding metal.

Yet another regiment of dragoons raised in 1715, the regiment became the 12th Prince of Wales's Light Dragoons in 1768 and it is from this association that the main device in the badge was drawn. The regiment was converted to lancers in 1816 and this change of role is reflected in the representation of crossed lances which form the background of the badge. While the badge dates from 1896, the above title was not adopted until 1921.

The 12th Lancers was converted to an armoured car regiment in 1926 and was one of the first cavalry regiments to land in France with the BEF in 1939. After the withdrawal from Dunkirk, it was transferred to North Africa in 1941 and ended the war in Northern Italy.

13TH/18TH ROYAL HUSSARS (QUEEN MARY'S OWN)

The monogram 'QMO' superimposed upon which is a scroll in the shape of a letter 'Z'. The top arm of the scroll rests on top of the monogram and is inscribed with the Roman numerals 'XIII'. The lower arm of the scroll supports the bottom of the monogram and is inscribed with the Roman numerals 'XVIIL'. The whole is ensigned with an Imperial Crown. The badge is in gilding metal.

The 13th/18th Royal Hussars was formed in 1922 by an amalgamation of the 13th Hussars which, like many of the early cavalry regiments, had been raised as dragoons in 1715, and the 18th Royal Hussars, which had been raised in 1759. The latter regiment had been given the title of 'Queen Mary's Own' in 1910 on the accession of King George V, which accounts for the monogram in the badge. The unusual scroll was adapted from that on the badge of the 13th Hussars.

After serving with the BEF in 1939–40, the 13th/18th withdrew to the UK returning to North West Europe in June 1944. It took part in the amphibious landings on D-Day and subsequently fought throughout the European Campaign, ending the war in Bremen.

14TH/20TH KING'S HUSSARS

The Prussian Eagle in gilding metal.

The 14th/20th King's Hussars was formed in 1922, from the amalgamation of two existing regiments: the 14th King's Hussars and the 20th Hussars. The first badge of the new regiment contained no allusion to either of the badges of the two regiments from which it had been formed. A most uninspiring badge, it was liked by personnel of neither tradition. Consequently, in 1931, the above badge, based on that of the 14th Hussars, was adopted.

The 14th King's Hussars was originally raised as Dormer's Dragoons in 1715 to combat the threat posed by the first Jacobite Rebellion. In 1798, it was granted the title of 14th (Duchess of York's Own) Light Dragoons in honour of Princess Frederica of Prussia who married the then Duke of York in 1791. Although the regiment's title was subsequently changed to the 14th King's Hussars, it retained its Prussian Eagle cap-badge which it had been given in honour of the Duchess of York. Like the 1st King's Dragoon Guards, the 14th Hussars was obliged to change its cap-badge in 1915 and thus discontinue its European connection.

The 20th Hussars, originally raised in Inniskilling in 1759, was, as a junior regiment of cavalry, subject to disbandment after each major conflict. However, in 1861, it was re-raised from a regiment of European cavalry in the East India Company's army and subsequently maintained an unbroken record of service until it was amalgamated with the 14th King's Hussars in 1922.

At the outbreak of the Second World War, the 14th/20th Hussars was serving in India from where it formed the spearhead of the invasion of Persia in 1941. It remained in the Middle East until the end of 1944 when it joined the Eighth Army in the Italian Campaign.

15TH/19TH THE KING'S ROYAL HUSSARS

The Royal Crest within the Garter and attached to the lower portion of the Garter, the Roman numerals 'XV' and 'XIX'. The bottom of the figures rest upon a scroll inscribed 'MEREBIMUR' (Let me be worthy). The Royal Crest is in white metal and the remainder of the badge is in gilding metal.

Badge backing. A scarlet outline was worn behind the badge to commemorate the fact that in 1799, King George III granted to the 15th Light Dragoons, the antecedents of the 15th Hussars, the special distinction of wearing a scarlet plume. The plume itself was replaced by a scarlet shako in 1812 and this, in turn, was replaced by a scarlet backing to the badge in 1888.

The 15th/19th The King's Royal Hussars was formed in 1922 from the 15th (The King's) Hussars and the 19th Queen Alexandra's Own Royal Hussars. The new regiment was originally simply titled the 15th/19th Hussars, but this was amended in December 1933 when the above designation was adopted. The 15th had been raised in 1759 as a regiment of light dragoons and was granted the title 'The King's' in 1766, becoming hussars in 1807. The 19th was raised in India in 1858 as the 1st Bengal Light Cavalry and was incorporated into the British Army as a hussar regiment in 1862. It was granted the title of Queen Alexandra's Own Royal Hussars by King Edward VII.

It is from the badge of the 15th Hussars, the senior of the two regiments, that the above badge is almost completely drawn, even down to the motto '*Merebimur*', which had been given to the regiment by King George III. The only change which occurred on amalgamation was the amendment to the figures on the scroll, which had previously read '*XV.KH*', to read '*XV.XIX*'.

The 15th/19th Hussars returned to North West Europe in August 1944, having had to withdraw with the remainder of the BEF after the Fall of France in 1940.

16TH/5TH LANCERS

On crossed lances with pennons flying outwards, the numeral '16' surmounted by an Imperial Crown. Below, a scroll inscribed 'THE QUEEN'S LANCERS'. The badge is in gilding metal, with the exception of the numeral, the scroll and the lower half of each pennon, all of which are in white metal.

The regiment was formed in 1922 from the 16th (Queen's Own) Lancers and the 5th (Royal Irish) Lancers. Although the 5th was founded in 1689, from troops which had defended Enniskillen, some seventy years before the 16th, it was disbanded for insubordination in 1799 and not reformed until 1858. It was thus the junior of the two regiments. The 16th was originally raised as light dragoons in 1759, given the title 'The Queen's' in 1766 and converted to lancers in 1816.

The badge of the 16th/5th, like many which were adopted in the 1922 amalgamations, is simply the badge of the senior of the two regiments, in this case the 16th Lancers.

The regiment was mechanised in 1939 when it joined the Royal Armoured Corps. It took part in the liberation of Tunisia and subsequently fought in the Italian Campaign.

17TH/21ST LANCERS

A pair of thigh bones crossed with a skull imposed thereon. Resting on the ends of the lower portions of the crossed bones, a scroll inscribed 'OR GLORY'. The badge is in white metal.

The badge of the 17th/21st Lancers was that of the 17th (The Duke of Cambridge's Own) Lancers, one of the two regiments amalgamated to form the 17th/21st in 1922. Both the 17th and the 21st had been raised as light dragoons, the 17th in 1759 and the 21st a year later. They were both converted to lancers in 1823, a role which the new regiment retained until mechanised in 1939.

The 17th Lancers had adopted the Death's Head as its badge from its foundation and, as the senior regiment, exercised the privilege of retaining its own badge after amalgamation.

The 17th/21st took part in the initial assault in Tunisia with the First Army in 1942 and after the completion of the North African Campaign continued in Italy until the German Army capitulated there in 1945.

22ND DRAGOONS

The capital letter 'D' surmounted by an Imperial Crown. Within the 'D', the Roman numeral 'XXII' and below it a scroll inscribed 'DRAGOONS'. The badge is in white metal.

Badge backing. The badge was backed by a green cloth diamond – the regimental colour of the 5th Royal Inniskilling Dragoon Guards – one of the regiments from which personnel were drawn to form the new regiment.

The 22nd Dragoons was one of six new cavalry regiments raised during the Second World War, all of which were formed from cadres provided by existing cavalry units. Like the more prosaically numbered regiments of the Royal Armoured Corps, the six regiments were not on the permanent establishment and this is probably why the new titles were adopted rather than restoring those of the cavalry regiments which had lost their original identities in 1922.

The 22nd Dragoons was the senior of the six, being raised in December 1940 and formed from cadres drawn from the 4th/7th Royal Dragoon Guards and the Royal Inniskilling Dragoon Guards. However, its unimaginative cap-badges reflects nothing of the regiment's parentage.

There had been previous regiments of the same name, but the 22nd Dragoons of the Second World War had no linear connection with them; the last regiment to carry the same title being disbanded in 1819.

The regiment served in the United Kingdom until 1944 when, equipped with flail tanks, it was one of the first units to land on the Normandy beaches on D-Day. It continued to see active service in North West Europe, before ending the war on the outskirts of Hamburg. The 22nd Dragoons was disbanded on 1st December 1945, five years to the day from the date of its formation.

23RD HUSSARS

The capital letter 'H' surmounted by an Imperial Crown. Below the 'H' is a scroll inscribed '23RD HUSSARS'. The 'H' is in white metal and the remainder of the badge is in gilding metal.

Badge backing. A domed green backing was worn behind the cap-badge, but there seems to be no reason why this, or indeed any, colour was chosen as backing.

Although there had been regiments with the same number in existence previously, the final cavalry regiment to bear the number 23 was the the 23rd Light Dragoons which had been disbanded in 1817, shortly after the end of the Napoleonic Wars.

Like the 22nd Dragoons, the 23rd Hussars was raised in December 1940 when the above, unprepossessing, badge was adopted. Formed initially from personnel from the 10th Royal Hussars and the 15th/19th Hussars, the regiment became part of the 11th Armoured Division in March 1941.

As part of that division, it landed in Normandy shortly after D-Day and ended the war on the shores of the Baltic, having fought throughout the North West Europe Campaign. After garrison duties in Schleswig-Holstein, the 23rd Hussars was disbanded in January 1946.

24TH LANCERS

A circlet inscribed in the lower portion '*LANCERS*'. Within the circlet and extending to its outer rim, a pair of crossed lances with the pennons flying outwards. Across the centre of the circlet and in front of the cross of the lances, the Roman numeral '*XXIV*'. The badge is in white metal.

Although mechanised from its inception, the 24th Lancers adopted a badge which, with crossed lances forming the main device, suggested an historical link with past cavalry traditions. However, no such connection existed. There had been a 24th Regiment of Light Dragoons which had been formed in 1804, but this had been disbanded shortly after the end of the Napoleonic Wars. In any event, because of its role, it would not have worn a badge associated with a regiment of lancers.

The 24th Lancers was raised in 1940 and remained in the United Kingdom until June 1944. The regiment took part in the Normandy Landings, but in the following month, owing to heavy casualties, it was disbanded and its personnel transferred to its sister regiment, the 23rd Hussars.

25TH DRAGOONS

A pair of crossed swords, points uppermost. On the cross of the swords, the Roman numeral '*XXV*'. Above the numeral and on the upper parts of the swords is an Imperial Crown. Below the numeral and above the handles of the swords, a scroll inscribed '*25TH DRAGOONS*'. The swords are in white metal and the remainder of the badge is in gilding metal.

The crossed swords, the main device of the badge, represent the historic arms of the dragoons, although the regiment's predecessor, the 25th Light Dragoons, did not use this device. Furthermore, there was no direct connection between the two regiments, as the original 25th had been disbanded as early as 1818.

The 25th Dragoons was raised in India in January 1941 from personnel of the 3rd Carabiniers. The regiment moved into the Arakan in November 1943 and fought in Burma until June 1944 after which it returned to India. Subsequently 'A' Squadron of the regiment returned to Burma in 1945 where it remained in action until the surrender of Japan in the August of that year.

26TH HUSSARS

The Prussian Eagle with a scroll below inscribed '*XXVI HUSSARS*'. The badge is in gilding metal.

Badge backing. A diamond patch, consisting of three vertical stripes, was worn behind the badge; the stripes from the left being: blue, a narrow yellow stripe and maroon.

The badge of the 26th Hussars was very similar to that of the 14th/20th Hussars from which its personnel were originally drawn.

Raised in India, like the 25th Dragoons, the 26th Hussars was originally part of the 23rd Indian Armoured Division. However, the regiment never saw any active service and was withdrawn from active duty in December 1943.

27TH LANCERS

A pair of crossed lances, pennons flying outwards. On the cross of the lances, an elephant head and within the upper portions of the lances, an Imperial Crown. Below the elephant's head, the figure '27'. The elephant's head and the lower part of the pennons are in white metal and the remainder of the badge is in gilding metal.

The badge is based on that of the 12th Lancers, drafts from which regiment formed the initial personnel of the 27th Lancers when it was raised in 1941. The elephant's head, which replaced the Prince of Wales's badge of the 12th Lancers, was taken from the badge of the 27th Light Dragoons which had been awarded the device for service in India. The original 27th, however, was disbanded shortly after the end of the Napoleonic Wars and the 27th Lancers not only had no lineal connection with it, but at no time in its short history did it ever serve in India.

Originally an armoured car regiment in the 11th Armoured Division, the regiment first saw active service in Egypt and the Western Desert. Later it was transferred to 10 Corps in Italy, but ended the war as part of the 6th Armoured Division which it led into Austria to face the advancing Russian forces.

THE ROYAL TANK REGIMENT

A laurel wreath surmounted by an Imperial Crown. Within the wreath, an early pattern tank facing left; on the bottom of the wreath a scroll inscribed '*FEAR NAUGHT*'. The badge is in white metal.

The Royal Tank Regiment traces its origins back to the Heavy Branch of the Machine Gun Corps which in July 1917 was formed into a separate unit – the Tank Corps. Personnel of the Heavy Branch of the MGC had worn a badge in the shape of a tank on the right sleeve of their uniform and on the formation of the Tank Corps, this device was adopted as its cap-badge.

The Tank Corps was granted the prefix 'Royal' in 1923 and a new badge, with the motto 'Fear Naught', was sealed in October 1924. With the formation of the Royal Armoured Corps in 1939, the title of the Royal Tank Corps was changed to the Royal Tank Regiment although there was no change to the cap-badge. However, the black beret which had been worn by the RTC, became the head-dress not only of the Royal Tank Regiment, but virtually all units in the Royal Armoured Corps.

Concurrently with the change in title, the eight yeomanry regiments, which had, as armoured car companies, been the Territorial Army components of the RTC, were expanded into regiments in their own right. They thus ceased to have any formal connection with the Royal Tank Regiment other than as fellow members of the Royal Armoured Corps.

The Royal Tank Regiment was expanded to twenty battalions during the Second World War. Of that number, twelve, the 40th to the 51st Battalions inclusive, had been infantry battalions and all, without exception, adopted the above badge on conversion.

THE NORTH IRISH HORSE

The Irish Harp ensigned with an Imperial Crown. Below the harp is a scroll inscribed 'NORTH IRISH HORSE'. The badge is in gilding metal.

In common with many other Irish regiments, the main device of the North Irish Horse was the Irish Harp, the distinguishing element being the identification on the scroll.

Although various yeomanry formations were raised in Ireland in the late eighteenth and early nineteenth centuries, they were not formed under the same legislation which covered the yeomanry in the rest of the United Kingdom. The North Irish Horse, therefore, had no historical traditions earlier than the South African War of 1900–92, after which two regiments of Imperial Yeomanry were formed in Ireland. On the formation of the Territorial Force in 1908, which did not extend to Ireland, the North Irish Imperial Yeomanry were transferred to the Special Reserve and re-designated the North Irish Horse. The above badge was adopted on the change of title.

As a Special Reserve regiment, the North Irish Horse took precedence after the Regular cavalry regiments and before the yeomanry.

The regiment was placed in suspended animation between the two world wars, but in May 1939 the North Irish Horse was re-activated as an armoured car regiment in the recently formed Royal Armoured Corps. Later it was equipped with tanks and saw active service in the Western Desert and Italian campaigns.

THE ROYAL WILTSHIRE YEOMANRY (PRINCE OF WALES'S OWN)

The Prince of Wales's plume, coronet and motto *'ICH DIEN'* (I Serve). The coronet is in gilding metal and the remainder of the badge is in white metal.

Badge backing. A rectangular scarlet patch was worn behind the badge.

The Royal Wiltshire Yeomanry was the senior yeomanry regiment, being originally raised in 1784. It was granted the prefix 'Royal' in 1831, the first yeomanry regiment to be so honoured, for its service during the 'Machine Riots' of 1830. The secondary title of the Prince of Wales's Own was granted in 1863, following the provision of an escort to the then Prince of Wales during a visit to Wiltshire, the first time a yeomanry regiment had been asked to undertake this task. The badge, which records this honour, dates from the award of this title.

The Royal Wiltshire Yeomanry continued as a horsed cavalry regiment between the two world wars and went to the Middle East in 1940 in that role. Subsequently it was mechanised as lorried infantry, and the regiment served in that role in the Iraq and Syrian campaigns. The Royal Wiltshire Yeomanry was then converted to armour and took part in the Battle of El Alamein. Suffering heavy losses it was withdrawn from the remainder of the North African Campaign but subsequently took part in operations in Italy.

THE WARWICKSHIRE YEOMANRY

The bear and ragged staff. The badge is in gilding metal.

The Warwickshire Yeomanry, originally raised in 1784 at the time of the French Revolution, was the second senior regiment of yeomanry. The badge was taken from the Arms of the Earl of Warwick and the same device also forms part of the crest of the Borough of Warwick.

The above cap-badge was worn throughout the Second World War in which most of the regiment's service was spent in the Middle East and Italy. Shortly after it was embodied in 1939, the Warwickshire Yeomanry was posted to Palestine from which base it took part in operations in Iraq and Syria as a cavalry unit.

It was not until 1941 that the Warwickshire Yeomanry was re-equipped with tanks when it joined the 2nd New Zealand Division in the Eighth Army and took part in the Battle of El Alamein. It subsequently fought in the remainder of the campaign in the Western Desert and in Italy.

THE YORKSHIRE HUSSARS
(ALEXANDRA, PRINCESS OF WALES'S OWN)

The White Rose of York surmounted by the Prince of Wales's plume, coronet and motto. The coronet is in gilding metal and the remainder of the badge is in white metal.

Badge backing. A red outline was worn behind the badge.

The third senior regiment of yeomanry, raised in the West Riding in 1794, it adopted the title of Hussars in the 1880s. The Yorkshire Hussars was given the secondary title of Alexandra, Princess of Wales's Own on the occasion of Queen Victoria's Diamond Jubilee in 1897 when the regiment took part in the Jubilee Parade. It is from this latter date that the above badge was worn, reflecting the regiment's association with both Yorkshire and the Princess of Wales.

A horsed cavalry regiment between the two world wars, the Yorkshire Hussars was sent out to the Middle East in 1940 as part of the 5th Cavalry Brigade. Converted to an armoured regiment in 1941, it fought in the North Africa Campaign until 1943 after which it returned to the United Kingdom.

THE NOTTINGHAMSHIRE
(SHERWOOD RANGERS) YEOMANRY

Within a strap inscribed '*NOTTS SHERWOOD RANGERS YEOMANRY*', a strung bugle. The whole is surmounted by an Imperial Crown. The badge is in gilding metal.

The Nottinghamshire Yeomanry was one of the original regiments of yeomanry raised at the time of the Napoleonic Wars and had subsequently been active in support of the civil power during the disturbances of the 1820s. It was for the stalwart service which it had displayed during these riots that the Nottinghamshire Yeomanry was exempted from disbandment in 1828.

In the same year, the then Colonel of the Regiment adopted for the regiment the name of 'Sherwood Rangers'. The name itself had been in use for at least thirty years previously by an infantry volunteer force which was absorbed into the yeomanry in 1828 and it is this which gave the regiment its badge. The strung bugle horn is identical to that worn by light infantry regiments which adopted it as emblematic of skirmishing or hunting. Presumably the Sherwood Rangers adopted it for the same reason when they were infantry volunteers.

The original badge was simply a strung bugle, the current badge with the inscribed strap and crown not being adopted until 1936.

Although the secondary title 'Sherwood Rangers' was adopted by the Nottinghamshire Yeomanry and appeared on its cap-badge, it was never officially recognised by the Army. In 1944, while the Nottinghamshire Yeomanry was engaged in North West Europe, there was an attempt by the War Office to regularise the position and moves were made to deprive the regiment of its secondary title. An appeal by the regiment to General Sir Brian Horrocks quickly quashed this bureaucratic interference with history.

The theatres in which the Nottinghamshire Yeomanly served in 1939–45 were matched by the variety of roles it was required to meet. Starting its active service as mounted cavalry in Palestine in July 1940, the regiment was converted briefly into coastal gunners and, as such, took part in the battle for Crete and the Siege of Tobruk. Converted to armour in late 1941, the Nottinghamshire Yeomanry fought throughout the Western Desert to the capture of Tunis. It was subsequently withdrawn to the United Kingdom and then took part in the North West Europe Campaign – the Reconnaissance Troop of the regiment being the first British troops to enter Germany.

Throughout these operations, the Nottinghamshire Yeomanry continued to wear the above badge.

THE STAFFORDSHIRE YEOMANRY
(QUEEN'S OWN ROYAL REGIMENT)

The Stafford Knot surmounted by a crown. The badge is in gilding metal.

Badge backing. On mechanisation of the regiment in 1941, officers of the Staffordshire Yeomanry adopted an inverted red triangle as backing to their badges, while Other Ranks wore a red circle. There is some controversy on the origin of the backing which was generally held to indicate the regiment's royal connection. However, it may be that the red triangle was chosen because the officer who suggested the backing had been a senior employee of the Bass Brewery in Burton! Whatever the reason, on transfer to North West Europe, the red backing ceased to be worn by both officers and men.

The Staffordshire Yeomanry was probably unique in that it had two cap-badges – the official pattern (left) and the unofficial, but preferred, pattern (on the right). The official badge with an Imperial Crown was sealed in 1916, but the unofficial one dated back to the reign of Queen Victoria, hence the Victorian crown. Each badge, however, bore the Stafford Knot as its main device. The Stafford Knot is derived from the Arms of the Stafford family and has been adopted by many organisations within the county, including both the County Council and the Borough of Stafford. In addition, the two Staffordshire County regiments incorporated the knot in their badges.

The Staffordshire Yeomanry was originally raised during the Napoleonic Wars and although it was mobilised several times during the nineteenth century in support of the civil power, it saw no active service until the Second Boer War. The regiment was given its secondary title of the Queen's Royal Regiment in 1838 by Queen Victoria in commemoration of its provision of a guard of honour when she visited Shugborough Hall and it has consequently worn the Victorian crown on its badge ever since.

Even during the height of the Second World War this tradition was maintained. On one occasion, when a draft of reinforcements was sent to the Western Desert to join the regiment, arrangements were made with a local Egyptian *fundi* to manufacture traditional badges for the new arrivals.

The Stafford Yeomanry was embodied as a horsed cavalry regiment in 1939 and was sent to Palestine. It subsequently fought in the Syrian Campaign before being mechanised in 1941, after which it was transferred to the Eighth Army and saw considerable action in the Western Desert. The regiment was withdrawn from the Middle East in 1943 to prepare for and take part in the North West Europe Campaign.

THE CHESHIRE (EARL OF CHESTER'S) YEOMANRY

The Prince of Wales's plume coronet and motto above a scroll inscribed 'CHESHIRE (EARL OF CHESTER'S) YEOMANRY'. The badge is in white metal and in bronze.

One of the senior regiments of yeomanry, the Cheshire Yeomanry was raised during the Napoleonic Wars and in 1803 the then Prince of Wales, as Earl of Chester, granted it permission to use his crest as its badge. The above title was granted in 1849 although the badge depicted was not adopted until after the Great War.

After embodiment in 1939, the Cheshire Yeomanry was sent to the Middle East serving as a horsed cavalry regiment in Palestine. The regiment took part in the invasion of Syria, then held by the Vichy French, where B Troop of the regiment had the distinction of taking part in the last cavalry charge of the British Army.

In March 1942 after the Syrian Campaign, the Cheshire Yeomanry was transferred to the Royal Corps of Signals, becoming the 5th (later, the 11th) Line of Communications Signals Regiment (Cheshire Yeomanry).

It subsequently saw further active service in the Western Desert, Italy and North West Europe with the Royal Corps of Signals, but retained the above badge throughout the Second World War.

THE QUEEN'S OWN YORKSHIRE DRAGOONS

The White Rose of York ensigned by an Imperial Crown. The badge is in gilding metal.

Originally raised in the West Riding in 1802, after several changes of name the regiment adopted the title of the Yorkshire Dragoons in 1889. However, following a visit of Queen Victoria to Sheffield in 1897 the title was altered to the Queen's Own Yorkshire Dragoons. The badge incorporated the White Rose and the crown to signify both the Yorkshire origins of the regiment and its royal association.

With the Yorkshire Hussars, the Yorkshire Dragoons formed part of the 5th Cavalry Brigade and was sent to the Middle East in 1940 where it served in Palestine and Syria. The regiment was subsequently converted to a motor battalion and took part in the Battle of El Alamein.

Late in 1942, it underwent a change of role and the Yorkshire Dragoons was re-designated as the 9th Battalion, the King's Own Yorkshire Light Infantry. However, it continued to wear the above badge.

THE NORTH SOMERSET YEOMANRY

A ten-pointed star, the topmost point being replaced by an Imperial Crown. In the centre is a circlet inscribed '*ARMA PACIS FULCRA*' (Arms, the mainstay of peace). Within the circlet, the cypher of King George VI. The badge is in white metal.

The first yeomanry unit in North Somerset was raised in Frome in 1789, but it was united in 1814 with other troops in the county to form the North Somerset Yeomanry. The above badge dates from the establishment of the Territorial Force in 1908 and the motto is one which is used by a number of yeomanry regiments, referring as it does to the role of the yeomanry as the first line of home defence.

The North Somerset Yeomanry retained its mounted role between the two world wars and it was as a horsed cavalry unit that it was sent to the Middle East in 1940. However, in 1942 the regiment converted to a signals role as the 4th Air Formation Signals Regiment and saw service in Sicily and Italy. In 1944 it was moved to North West Europe and on its transfer it was re-designated 14th Air Formation Signals Regiment.

Despite these changes, the North Somerset Yeomanry continued to wear its original badge.

THE DERBYSHIRE YEOMANRY

A rose within a laurel wreath surmounted by an Imperial Crown. On the wreath are scrolls inscribed 'SOUTH AFRICA 1900, 1901'. Below are two scrolls inscribed 'DERBYSHIRE YEOMANRY' and between the scrolls is a tablet on which there is a sprig of laurel. The badge is white metal.

Raised in 1830 to combat the threat of civil unrest, the Derbyshire Yeomanry traced its origins back some thirty years earlier to the Napoleonic Wars. The regiment first saw action when, as the Derbyshire Imperial Yeomanry, it served in the Second Boer War for which it was granted the battle honour 'South Africa 1900, 1901' and which appears on the wreath round the Derbyshire Rose in the badge. While the rose had been in use prior to the formation of the Imperial Yeomanry, the above badge dates from the formation of the Territorial Force in 1908. The main change which occurred in the badge then was that the word 'Imperial' was removed from the tablet below the rose and replaced with the sprig of laurel.

After the Great War, the Derbyshire Yeomanry became the 24th Armoured Car Company of the Royal Tank Corps (TA), but in 1938 it was expanded into two regiments, the 1st and 2nd Derbyshire Yeomanry, both of which wore the above badge.

The 1st Derbyshire Yeomanry began its active service in North Africa, being the first British troops into Tunis and then went into the Italian Campaign where, for a time, it was employed as infantry. It subsequently led the advance north from Monte Cassino and ended the war in Austria.

The 2nd Derbyshire Yeomanry also first saw action in North Africa but in 1943 it was withdrawn to the United Kingdom to prepare for the invasion of Europe. It was transferred to the Reconnaissance Corps in late 1944 but, almost uniquely, continued to wear its own badge.

THE ROYAL GLOUCESTERSHIRE HUSSARS

A portcullis with chains surmounted by a ducal crown. Below the portcullis is a scroll inscribed '*ROYAL GLOUCESTERSHIRE HUSSARS*'. The badge is in gilding metal.

The badge of the regiment was based on the coat of arms of the Duke of Beaufort who had been closely associated with the Royal Gloucestershire Hussars since its formation in 1834.

After the First World War, the Royal Gloucestershire Hussars was reformed as an Armoured Car Company of the Royal Tank Corps (TA). In 1939, it was expanded into two regiments and transferred to the Royal Armoured Corps.

While the 1st Royal Gloucestershire Hussars became a training regiment and remained in the United Kingdom during the Second World War, the 2nd was sent to North Africa to join the Eighth Army. After taking part in a number of earlier operations, the regiment was badly mauled in the Battles of Knightsbridge and Sidi Barrani. The 2nd Royal Gloucestershire Hussars was subsequently disbanded and its survivors posted to other regiments.

Both regiments wore the above badge.

THE LOTHIANS AND BORDER HORSE

A garb (a sheaf of wheat). The badge is in gilding metal.

The first yeomanry unit in Lothian was the East Lothian Yeomanry, raised in 1797, and the sheaf of wheat associated with the farming lands of the county was used as the regiment's badge. When the Lothians and Border Horse was re-designated in 1908 on the formation of the Territorial Force, the same badge was adopted.

Reduced to an armoured car company after the Great War, the Lothians and Border Horse, like many other yeomanry regiments, was expanded into two regiments in 1939. Although the two regiments were recorded in the Army List as the Lothians and Border Horse, each regiment adopted its own version of the title. The first line regiment adopted the title 'The Lothian and Border Yeomanry', the second regiment simply taking the title of 'The Lothians and Border Horse'.

Both regiments went to France with the BEF in 1939. The 1st Lothians, with the 51st Highland Division and with the remains of that division, were captured at St Valery en Caux. Three officers and seventeen NCOs and other ranks escaped and formed the basis of the new 1st Lothians. This regiment remained in the United Kingdom until 1944 when it returned to Normandy and served throughout the North West Europe Campaign. Because of their part in the defence of St Valery four years earlier, Field Marshal Montgomery gave the regiment the honour of relieving the town in 1944.

The 2nd Lothians were withdrawn through Dunkirk with the remnants of the BEF in 1940. They next saw action when, as part of the British First Army, they landed in Algeria in 1942. After the completion of the North African Campaign, the regiment took part in the Italian Campaign until the collapse of Germany in 1945

Despite the difference in their titles, both regiments continued to wear the same badge.

THE FIFE AND FORFAR YEOMANRY

The Thane of Fife. The badge is in white metal.

The Fife and Forfar Yeomanry was able to trace its origins back to the Kirkaldy Troop of Yeomanry raised in 1797. However, the regiment was only established on the formation of the Territorial Force in 1908 when the Fife Mounted Rifles and the Forfar Light Horse were amalgamated and the above badge adopted. The Thane of Fife is the County badge of Fife and had previously been used by the Fife Mounted Rifles in its cap-badge as early as 1864.

Between the two world wars, the regiment was reduced to company strength, becoming 20th Armoured Car Company, Royal Tank Corps (TA). Expanding rapidly in 1939, the Fife and Forfar Yeomanry formed two divisional cavalry regiments equipped with light tanks.

The 1st Fife and Forfar Yeomanry went to France with the 51st (Highland) Division in January 1940 but after the withdrawal of the BEF from France, it was transferred to the 79th Armoured Division in which it fought in the later stages of the North West Europe Campaign.

The second regiment landed in Normandy in June 1944 with 11th Armoured Division and was involved throughout the North West Europe Campaign, ending the war in Lubeck.

Both regiments wore the above badge.

2ND COUNTY OF LONDON YEOMANRY (THE WESTMINSTER DRAGOONS)

The arms of the City of Westminster, below which is a scroll inscribed '*WESTMINSTER DRAGOONS TY*'. The badge is white metal.

The regiment was originally raised in 1901 as a regiment of Imperial Yeomanry. It was given the secondary title of Westminster Dragoons in 1903, having adopted the coat of arms of the City of Westminster as its badge on its formation. On the formation of the Territorial Force in 1908, the Imperial Yeomanry regiments dropped 'Imperial' from their titles and their badges were altered accordingly. In the case of the Westminster Dragoons' badge, the initials 'IY' in the centre of the scroll under the arms of Westminster were replaced by 'TY'.

After the First World War the regiment re-formed as the 22nd (London) Armoured Car Company, Royal Tank Corps (TA), but in 1937 it was raised to battalion strength as 22nd Battalion (Westminster Dragoons) Royal Tank Corps as an officer cadet training unit subsequently becoming, in 1939, the 102nd Officer Cadet Training Unit (Westminster Dragoons). In 1940 it was re-established as an active service regiment and was transferred to the Royal Armoured Corps as the 2nd County of London Yeomanry (Westminster Dragoons).

It was later issued with flail tanks and, after landing in Normandy on D-Day, fought throughout the North West Europe Campaign.

3RD COUNTY OF LONDON YEOMANRY (THE SHARPSHOOTERS)

A circlet inscribed '*COUNTY OF LONDON YEOMANRY*' and surmounted by an Imperial Crown. In the centre of the circlet, the letters '*CLY*', the whole superimposed on crossed rifles. Below the circlet, a scroll inscribed '*SHARPSHOOTERS*'. The letters 'CLY' are in white metal and the remainder of the badge is in gilding metal.

The 3rd County of London Imperial Yeomanry was formed in 1901 from veterans of the South African War. The regiment's title was amended on the formation of the Territorial Force, when the word 'Imperial' was dropped from the designation of all yeomanry regiments. Its secondary title, 'The Sharpshooters', was given to the regiment because of the high level of marksmanship which had to be demonstrated by would-be recruits.

Reduced to company strength after the Great War as the 23rd (London) Armoured Car Company of the Royal Tank Corps (TA), the regiment expanded to full strength in 1938. In November 1939 the War Office issued an instruction to all TA units incorporated into the Royal Armoured Corps advising them that their cap-badges should revert to the pattern worn prior to their conversion to armoured car companies. The 3rd County of London Yeomanry did not accede to this requirement; instead its Armoured Car Company badge was adapted and worn until the above badge was approved by the War Office in June 1940.

The Sharpshooters arrived in the Middle East in October 1941 and subsequently fought in the Western Desert, Sicily and Italy. It was withdrawn from the Italian Campaign to prepare for the invasion of North West Europe, landing in Normandy in June 1944. However, it suffered heavy losses in July, as did the 4th CLY, and at the end of that month the two regiments were temporarily withdrawn from the front line and formally amalgamated as the 3/4th County of London Yeomanry, retaining the above badge.

4TH COUNTY OF LONDON YEOMANRY (THE SHARPSHOOTERS)

A circlet inscribed 'COUNTY OF LONDON YEOMANRY' and surmounted by an Imperial Crown. In the centre of the circlet the numeral '4', the whole superimposed on crossed rifles. Below is a scroll inscribed 'SHARPSHOOTERS'. The numeral is in white metal and the remainder of the badge is in gilding metal.

The 4th County of London Yeomanry was raised as a duplicate regiment of the 3rd County of London Yeomanry on the expansion of the Territorial Army in 1939. However, there was little in common between the new 4th and its parent 3rd, the differences being reflected in their badges.

Thus although the cap-badge for both regiments was that approved by the War Office in June 1940 and adopted by the 3rd CLY, the 4th County of London Yeomanry continued to wear the above badge, based on that of the 23rd Armoured Car Company, and which had been unofficially introduced on the formation of the regiment. Because it was never officially recognised, the badge was manufactured locally, which accounts for the differences which may be found in the design of the figure '4' in the centre of the badge.

The County of London Yeomanry was brigaded with its parent regiment and went to Egypt in October 1941. After fighting through North Africa and Italy, it was withdrawn to England to prepare for Operation Overlord. Following heavy fighting in the early days of the campaign, in Normandy in which the regiment sustained very heavy losses, the 4th CLY was amalgamated with the 3rd CLY and the unofficial cap-badge ceased to be worn.

The new regiment continued to take a leading part in the Allied advance through the Netherlands and into Germany, ending the war in Hamburg.

1ST NORTHAMPTONSHIRE YEOMANRY

The White Horse of Hanover on ground. The badge is in white metal.

Badge backing. A royal blue circular patch was worn behind the badge.

Although there had been regiments of yeomanry raised in Northamptonshire during the Napoleonic era, none had had a continuous existence. The Northamptonshire Yeomanry was, therefore, only able to trace its direct lineage back to the Northamptonshire Imperial Yeomanry which had been raised for service in the Second Boer War. The Northamptonshire Imperial Yeomanry had adopted the White Horse of Hanover as its badge, although there appears to be no historic reason for the choice of device. On the formation of the Territorial Force, when the Imperial Yeomanry regiments were re-named, the new Northamptonshire Yeomanry amended the badge of its predecessor, dispensing with the oval on which the title of the regiment had been inscribed.

After service in the Great War, the Northamptonshire Yeomanry formed the 25th Armoured Car Company of the Royal Tank Corps (TA), but like all the other Armoured Car Companies it became a regiment in its own right on the expansion of the Territorial Army in 1939, at which juncture it re-assumed the above title.

In addition, a second regiment was raised. However, the 2nd Northamptonshire Yeomanry (*qv*) adopted a different badge which was more closely patterned on that of the Imperial Yeomanry.

Both regiments joined the 20th Armoured Division, but in 1943 on its disbandment, the 1st Northamptonshire Yeomanry was transferred to the 33rd Independent Armoured Brigade. It took part in the invasion of Normandy, fought into the Netherlands and, after the Battle of the Bulge in the Ardennes, was involved in the Rhine crossing into Germany.

2ND NORTHAMPTONSHIRE YEOMANRY

The White Horse of Hanover within an oval inscribed 'NORTHAMPTONSHIRE YEOMANRY'. The badge is in white metal.

Badge backing. A royal blue insert was worn within the oval of the badge.

The 2nd Northamptonshire Yeomanry was raised in April 1939 during the expansion of the Territorial Army. It took its badge from that of the Northamptonshire Imperial Yeomanry, merely omitting the word 'Imperial' from the title on the oval of the badge. Like the 1st Northamptonshire Yeomanry, the 2nd adopted a royal blue embellishment to its badge, but there appears to be no reason why this colour was chosen.

The regiment served with 20th Armoured Division until 1943, when it was transferred to the 11th Armoured Division and took part in the invasion of Normandy. After taking part in the Battle of Caen, the regiment suffered very heavy casualties in the battle to effect the crossing of the River Orme. Further heavy casualties in August 1944 led to the disbandment of the 2nd Northamptonshire Yeomanry, the survivors being transferred to either the 1st Northamptonshire Yeomanry or the 8th Hussars.

THE EAST RIDING OF YORKSHIRE YEOMANRY

A fox in full cry. Below a scroll inscribed 'FORRARD'. The fox is in gilding metal and the scroll is in white metal.

Although there were yeomanry units raised in the East Riding during the Napoleonic Wars, none survived through the nineteenth century. The East Riding Yeomanry was derived from the East Riding Imperial Yeomanry raised for service in South Africa during the Second Boer War. In 1908, when the Imperial Yeomanry units were absorbed into the newly formed Territorial Force, the cap-badge of the East Riding Yeomanry was changed to reflect the new title. The original badge of the East Riding Imperial Yeomanry had simply been a fox in full cry, which reflected the fox-hunting traditions of the landowners and farmers who were the mainstay of the regiment. On the change of name, the scroll with its motto, which itself is part of a hunting cry, was added.

Re-formed after the First World War as the 16th Armoured Car Company of the RTC, in 1939 the East Riding Yeomanry was expanded into two regiments which were subsequently incorporated into the Royal Armoured Corps.

The 1st East Riding Yeomanry served in the United Kingdom until June 1944 when it took part in the Normandy landings. It subsequently fought throughout the North West Europe Campaign.

The 2nd East Riding Yeomanry did not survive long as an armoured regiment. It was first converted to an infantry battalion as the 10th Battalion, The Green Howards, and then in 1942 it became the 12th Battalion, The Parachute Regiment. On each occasion it adopted the cap-badge of its new regiment.

THE INNS OF COURT REGIMENT

Within a laurel wreath surmounted by an Imperial Crown, four shields placed in the form of a cross, the points of the shields meeting in the centre. Each shield bears the arms of one of the Inns of Court. From the top and proceeding clockwise the coats of arms are: Lincoln's Inn (a number of millrinds with a lion rampant in the upper left quadrant), Inner Temple (Pegasus), Gray's Inn (a Griffin) and, finally, Middle Temple (St George's Cross with a Paschal Lamb in the centre of the cross). On the wreath are scrolls inscribed '*SOUTH AFRICA 1900–1901*'. Below the wreath is a second scroll inscribed '*INNS OF COURT REGT*'. The badge is in gilding metal.

The Inns of Court first raised a volunteer corps in 1584 and the unit has had a continuous existence ever since although, inevitably, there have been several changes of title.

After service in the Boer War, where it obtained the battle honour displayed on its badge, the regiment became the Inns of Court Officers' Training Corps in 1908. As such, it served throughout the Great War and for the greater part of the inter-war years. Its title changed in 1932 when it became the Inns of Court Regiment and its cap-badge was altered to reflect this change. Despite the change of name, the regiment continued to act as an officer training unit for the Territorial Army. However, shortly after the outbreak of the Second World War, the Inns of Court Regiment ceased to be a training unit and was transferred to the Royal Armoured Corps as an armoured car regiment.

The regiment remained in the United Kingdom until June 1944 when it was involved in the Normandy landings and subsequently fought through to the surrender of Germany.

INFANTRY BATTALIONS

which served with

THE ROYAL ARMOURED CORPS

Of the thirty-three infantry battalions which were converted to armour and served in the Royal Armoured Corps in the period 1941–42, the following continued to wear the badges of the infantry regiments from which they were drawn, even though they wore the black beret of the RAC:

107th Regiment	5th Bn	The King's Own Royal Regiment
108th Regiment	1/5th Bn	The Lancashire Fusiliers
109th Regiment	1/6th Bn	The Lancashire Fusiliers
110th Regiment	6th Bn	The Border Regiment
112th Regiment	9th Bn	The Sherwood Foresters
141st Regiment	7th Bn	The Buffs (Royal East Kent Regiment)
142nd Regiment	7th Bn	The Suffolk Regiment
143rd Regiment	9th Bn	The Lancashire Fusiliers
144th Regiment	8th Bn	The East Lancashire Regiment
147th Regiment	10th Bn	The Hampshire Regiment
153rd Regiment	8th Bn	The Essex Regiment
155th Regiment	15th Bn	The Durham Light Infantry
156th Regiment	11th Bn	The Highland Light Infantry
160th Regiment	9th Bn	The Royal Sussex Regiment
162nd Regiment	9th Bn	The Queen's Own Royal West Kent Regt
163rd Regiment	13th Bn	The Sherwood Foresters

Details of their badges are given in Section VI.

In addition, all the regiments of the Reconnaissance Corps, which was transferred to the RAC in 1944, continued to wear their own badges.

SECTION III

THE ROYAL ARTILLERY

THE ROYAL REGIMENT OF ARTILLERY

Two badges were worn:

left. A muzzle-loading gun on ground. Above the gun, a scroll inscribed *'UBIQUE'* (Everywhere) and ensigned with an Imperial Crown. Below the gun is a second scroll inscribed *'QUO FAS ET GLORIA DUCUNT'* (Where Right and Glory lead). The badge is in gilding metal.

right. A grenade with seven flames with, below, a scroll inscribed *'UBIQUE'*. This badge is also in gilding metal.

The first badge, which symbolises the role of the Royal Regiment of Artillery was adopted in 1833 while the two mottoes, which in themselves reflect the need for artillery in every theatre of war, were granted in the previous year.

The second cap-badge, which is also symbolic of artillery, was introduced during the Second World War for use when the FS cap was worn.

Following the development of both artillery and mechanised transport in the First World War, it was obvious that there would be a much smaller need for cavalry in any future conflicts. As a result, a large number of yeomanry units were required to convert to either armour or artillery when the Territorial Army was re-organised in 1921. The majority of yeomanry units chose to become gunners, largely because they felt that they would have an opportunity to remain mounted. However, that illusion was quickly shattered, for by 1927, the first of the yeomanry artillery regiments had been mechanised.

Army Council Instruction 414 of 1921 gave yeomanry regiments which converted to artillery three options in respect of their insignia:

a. to retain their old cap-badges and buttons
b. to adopt the cap-badges and buttons of the Royal Artillery
c. to adopt new cap-badges and buttons which would incorporate their own devices with that of the Royal Artillery. (Only one regiment, the Royal Devonshire Yeomanry Artillery, opted for this course of action)

In addition to the three official choices there was a fourth, unofficial, option which a number of regiments took – that of adopting the cap-badge of the RA while retaining their own buttons. The decision on which cap-badge to adopt appears to have been left to the regiments' discretion and, in many cases, to that of their then commanding officers.

During the late 1930s, as the possibility of a Second World War drew ominously closer, there were two further waves of conversions to artillery, one involving Territorial infantry battalions and the other involving more yeomanry regiments.

Initially, in 1936 a number of the former were transferred to the Royal Engineers as searchlight units, but whether they enjoyed their spell in the Royal Engineers or not, no less than sixty-seven former infantry battalions were converted to artillery regiments in 1940 when all anti-aircraft defences were coordinated within the Royal Artillery. Again, the same lack of uniformity which the yeomanry had experienced in the previous decade applied to the choice of badges which these new regiments wore, although whether the retention of the infantry badges was official or not does not appear to be clear.

In the expansion of the Territorial Army in 1938/9, many yeomanry regiments were doubled and further increased the number of regiments in the Royal Artillery. However, not all the duplicate formations followed the pattern of their parent regiments in retaining their yeomanry badges.

All in all, over eight hundred regiments of artillery were raised in the Second World War serving in every campaign from France in 1939 to the defeat of the Japanese in the Far East in 1945.

THE ROYAL HORSE ARTILLERY

Two badges were worn:

a. The badge of the Royal Artillery (*qv*).

b. The Royal Cypher of King George VI within the Garter and surmounted by an Imperial Crown. Below is a scroll inscribed '*ROYAL HORSE ARTILLERY*'. The badge is in white metal.

Although the Royal Horse Artillery was formed in 1793, it wore the normal Royal Artillery badge until 1935 when the second badge was introduced. Even then, this latter badge was only worn in India – by E Troop of No 1 Regiment RHA. However, it was unofficially adopted by other regiments in the RHA during the Second World War for use in the cap GS. Otherwise the normal Royal Artillery badge continued to be worn.

Like the Royal Artillery, the RHA was progressively mechanised in the period between the two world wars. During the Second World War it expanded to no less than fourteen regiments, including eight Territorial and yeomanry formations. Some of the latter continued to wear their own cap-badges and these are described later in this section.

As may be expected, the Royal Horse Artillery saw active service in all major theatres of war, ranging from North West Europe to the Far East.

THE HONOURABLE ARTILLERY COMPANY
(Artillery Division)

served as
86th (HAC) Heavy Anti-Aircraft Regiment RA
11th (HAC) Regiment RHA
12th (HAC) Regiment RHA
13th (HAC) Regiment RHA
121st (HAC) Officer Cadet Training Unit

An old-fashioned cannon on ground, with a scroll above inscribed '*HAC*' and above the scroll an Imperial Crown. Below the cannon is a second scroll inscribed '*ARMA PACIS FULCRA*' (Arms, the mainstay of peace). The badge is in gilding metal.

The Honourable Artillery Company traces its origins back to 1537 when it was granted a charter by King Henry VIII and has, therefore, the longest continuous history of any British military formation. The HAC has always been a volunteer unit, but it was not until 1871 that it was re-organised into two divisions, one artillery and one infantry. The badge of the artillery component is an adaptation of that of the Royal Artillery.

In 1938, the Artillery Division of the HAC consisted merely of a two-battery regiment of the Royal Horse Artillery (TA). The expansion of the Territorial Army in 1939 saw these two batteries expanded initially into three regiments, while later that year, a fourth regiment was formed from a cadre of one of the new units. Of the four regiments, three were incorporated into the Royal Horse Artillery, while the fourth became a heavy anti-aircraft regiment. In addition, the Artillery Division also formed the 121st Officer Cadet Training Unit.

All the units derived from the Honourable Artillery company wore the above badge.

THE SHROPSHIRE YEOMANRY

served as

75th (Shropshire Yeomanry) Medium Regiment RA
76th (Shropshire Yeomanry) Medium Regiment RA

Three leopards' faces within a strap inscribed '*SHROPSHIRE YEOMANRY*' surmounted by an Imperial Crown. The badge is in gilding metal.

The three leopards' faces ('loggerheads') which form the main device of the badge are taken from the arms of the county town of Shrewsbury in which they first appeared in the fifteenth century.

The Shropshire Yeomanry traced its existence back to the Napoleonic Wars when a number of troops of yeomanry were raised in the county. Through successive amalgamations these were unified into the Shropshire Cavalry Yeomanry in 1872 when the above badge was introduced. The regiment served in the Second Boer War as the Shropshire Imperial Yeomanry, adopting the above title on the formation of the Territorial Force in 1908. After distinguished service in the Great War, the Shropshire Yeomanry was re-formed as a horsed cavalry regiment in 1920.

It was embodied as such in September 1939, but in January 1940 the regiment lost its horses and was converted to gunners. 'A' and HQ Squadrons formed the nucleus of the 75th Medium Regiment RA, while 'B' and 'C' Squadrons undertook the same role for the 76th Medium Regiment. Despite the change in role, both regiments continued to wear the yeomanry badge.

After active service in various parts of the Middle East, the two regiments moved to Italy in 1943 serving, at different times, in both the 5th and 8th Armies. Both the 75th and 76th ended the war on the north east frontier of Italy to protect it against possible encroachments by the Jugoslav Communists.

THE AYRSHIRE YEOMANRY
(THE EARL OF CARRICK'S OWN)

served as
151st (Ayrshire Yeomanry) Field Regiment RA
152nd (Ayrshire Yeomanry) Field Regiment RA

The Crest of the Earl of Carrick (a Griffin with a lion's head, flaming tongue and eagle's wings on a torse). Below, a scroll inscribed *'AYRSHIRE EARL OF CARRICK'S OWN YEOMANRY'*. The badge is in gilding metal.

The Ayrshire Yeomanry was formed in 1803 from a number of Troops of Yeomanry which had already been raised in the county and was given its secondary title in 1897 to mark the Golden Jubilee of Queen Victoria. The title, the Earl of Carrick, is one of the hereditary titles of the heir to the throne, and it is from his coat of arms that the badge of the Ayrshire Yeomanry is derived.

Re-formed as a cavalry regiment after the Great War, the Ayrshire Yeomanry was converted to artillery in 1940 when it formed the 151st and 152nd Field Regiments RA. Both regiments retained the above badge.

The 151st Field Regiment remained in England until June 1944 when it landed in Normandy with the 11th Armoured Division and fought throughout the North West Europe Campaign. The 152nd Field Regiment was sent to North Africa in 1942. After extensive action in the Western Desert, the regiment was engaged in the Italian Campaign from February 1944 until the Germans surrendered in May 1945.

THE LEICESTERSHIRE YEOMANRY (PRINCE ALBERT'S OWN)

served as
153rd (Leicestershire Yeomanry) Field Regiment RA
154th (Leicestershire Yeomanry) Field Regiment RA

The crest of Albert, Prince Consort, with, above, a scroll inscribed 'LEICESTERSHIRE' and a further scroll below inscribed 'PRINCE ALBERT'S OWN YEOMANRY'. Below the second scroll is a lower scroll inscribed 'SOUTH AFRICA 1900–1902'. The badge is in gilding metal.

The Leicestershire Light Horse, from which the regiment claims its origins, was raised in 1744 but disbanded in 1802. It was raised again the following year and served continuously until the post-Second World War amalgamations. In 1844, the Leicestershire Yeomanry was granted the secondary title of Prince Albert's Own, hence the main device of the badge. It provided two companies of Imperial Yeomanry in the South African War for which it was granted the battle honour shown.

The Leicestershire Yeomanry remained as a mounted cavalry regiment between the two world wars and was mobilised as such in 1939. In August 1940, the regiment was converted to artillery forming the 153rd and 154th Field Regiments RA. Both regiments, however, continued to wear the Yeomanry badge.

153rd Field Regiment became part of the Guards Armoured Division and fought with that division throughout the North West Europe Campaign. The 154th Regiment served in the Middle East and North Africa. It subsequently landed in Italy and served there until the end of hostilities with Germany.

THE DUKE OF LANCASTER'S OWN YEOMANRY

served as
77th (DLOY) Medium Regiment RA
78th (DLOY) Medium Regiment RA

A rose within a wreath composed of laurel leaves on the left of the rose and oak leaves on the right. On the wreath are scrolls inscribed '*DUKE OF LANCASTER'S OWN*', the whole surmounted by a ducal coronet. The badge is in gilding metal.

The main device of the badge was a rose representing the Red Rose of Lancaster while the ducal coronet signified the regiment's association with the Duke of Lancaster – one of the monarch's personal titles. The wreath was unusual consisting, as it did, of a representation of two different types of leaf although there appeared to be no historical significance for this choice.

The regiment was raised in 1819 and since 1834 the reigning sovereign has always been its colonel-in-chief.

After service in the Great War as an infantry regiment, the Duke of Lancaster's Own Yeomanry was re-formed as a horsed cavalry unit in 1920. In 1940, however, the regiment was converted to artillery, forming the 77th and 78th Medium Regiments RA. Both regiments were permitted to wear the yeomanry badge as long as pre-war stocks lasted and it seems that DLOY badges remained 'available' virtually throughout the war, so that relatively few personnel ever wore the RA badge.

The 77th Regiment remained in the United Kingdom until shortly after D-Day when it landed in France and fought throughout the North West Europe Campaign. The 78th served in the Italian Campaign, including the assault on Monte Cassino.

THE LANARKSHIRE YEOMANRY

served as
155th (Lanarkshire Yeomanry) Field Regiment RA
156th (Lanarkshire Yeomanry) Field Regiment RA

A double-headed eagle grasping a bell in its right talon, the whole surmounted by an Imperial Crown. Below the eagle is a scroll inscribed 'LANARKSHIRE YEOMANRY'. The badge is in gilding metal.

The badge was based on the coat of arms of the Royal Burgh of Lanark which has borne the double-headed eagle since the fifteenth century.

Raised in 1819, the Lanarkshire Yeomanry had a continuous existence until the post-Second World War amalgamations. After service in the First World War in an infantry role, the Lanarkshire Yeomanry was re-formed as horsed cavalry in 1920 and remained as such until it was converted to artillery in 1940. It was then divided into two regiments but both continued to wear the above badge.

155th Field Regiment, less one battery, was sent to Malaya in September 1941 and was lost in the Japanese invasion. The remaining battery joined 160th Field Regiment and fought in the Arakan and Burma campaigns.

The 156th Regiment served throughout the Middle East, including the campaigns in Persia, Syria and the Western Desert before being committed to action in Sicily and Italy. However, it was withdrawn from Italy in 1944 and returned to Palestine for the remainder of the war.

THE NORTHUMBERLAND HUSSARS

served as
102nd (Northumberland Hussars) Light Anti-Tank Regiment RA
274th (Northumberland Hussars) Light Anti-Aircraft Battery RA

A circlet inscribed 'NORTHUMBERLAND HUSSARS' ensigned with an Imperial Crown: within the circlet, a representation of the Norman castle from the Arms of Newcastle-upon-Tyne. Below the circlet is a scroll inscribed 'SOUTH AFRICA 1900–1902'. The badge is found in either gilding metal or white metal.

Originally raised in 1797 in Newcastle, hence the representation of the castle in the badge, the Northumberland Hussars first saw active service in the Second Boer War in which it provided units of Imperial Yeomanry. It was due to service in that war that the regiment received its first battle honour which appears on the scroll below the badge.

In 1939 the regiment was required to convert to artillery and was given the option of becoming an anti-tank or field artillery unit. Whatever the option, the War Office agreed that the regiment could continue to wear its own badge and that the words 'Northumberland Hussars' would appear in the title of the new formation. The regiment opted for an anti-tank role but, in addition, was given an anti-aircraft responsibility. Initially, therefore, it was designated 102nd (Northumberland Hussars) Light Anti-Aircraft and Anti-Tank Regiment TA.

In November 1940, the Northumberland Hussars sailed for the Middle East as part of the 2nd Armoured Division, A and B Batteries being equipped in an anti-aircraft role and C and D Batteries as anti-tank. However, the Middle East establishment allowed an armoured division to contain one anti-tank regiment of three batteries and a separate anti-aircraft battery. As a result, B Battery became an anti-tank battery and remained a constituent part of the regiment.

A Battery remained in an anti-aircraft role and became 274 (Northumberland Hussars) Light Anti-Aircraft Battery RA. Although it was eventually incorporated into the 25th Light Anti-Aircraft Regiment in November 1941, it still retained its title and badge.

With B, C and D Batteries continuing in an anti-tank role, the name of the regiment was amended slightly to reflect this, becoming simply the 102nd (Northumberland Hussars) Light Anti-Tank Regiment RA.

Sent to Greece in 1941, the Northumberland Hussars suffered heavily in the fall of Crete and was not reformed until 1942, after which it saw service in the Western Desert.

THE SOUTH NOTTINGHAMSHIRE HUSSARS

served as
107th (South Nottinghamshire Hussars Yeomanry) Regiment RHA
150th (South Nottinghamshire Hussars Yeomanry) Field Regiment RA

A slip of oak with acorn. The badge is found in gilding metal or white metal.

The Nottingham Troop of Yeomanry Cavalry was first raised in July 1794 during the Napoleonic Wars and, together with other troops in the county it was formed, in 1826, into the Southern Regiment of Nottinghamshire Yeomanry Cavalry. By the 1880s the regiment had become known locally as the South Nottinghamshire Hussars but this title was not officially bestowed until 1902.

The badge is a derivation of the county badge of Nottinghamshire – an oak tree – but was not adopted until 1898, before which the regiment had simply used the monogram SNH.

After the Great War, the South Notts Hussars converted to artillery and eventually became 107th Regiment, the Royal Horse Artillery, although the change-over from horse to MT took place as early as 1932.

In 1939, the regiment raised a duplicate unit, but this later became a field regiment as the 150th (South Nottinghamshire Hussars Yeomanry) Field Regiment RA. However, both regiments wore the 'acorn' badge throughout the Second World War.

The 107th Regiment embarked for the Middle East in 1940 and, after taking part in the siege of Tobruk in 1941, was severely mauled at the Battle of Knightsbridge in June 1942. The remnants of the regiment formed a medium battery and, as such, took part in the later stages of the campaign in the Western Desert as well as in Sicily and the invasion of Italy. It returned to England in 1943 and re-formed as a medium regiment to take part in the North West Europe Campaign from Normandy to the fall of Germany.

The 150th Field Regiment served in the United Kingdom until 1944, when it, too, was involved in the invasion of France, landing in Normandy shortly alter D-Day. However, it was disbanded in November 1944.

THE HAMPSHIRE CARABINIERS YEOMANRY

served as
217th (Hampshire Carabiniers) Heavy Anti-Aircraft Battery RA

The Hampshire Rose within an oval inscribed '*HAMPSHIRE YEOMANRY*' ensigned by an Imperial Crown. Behind the oval are crossed carbines across the stocks of which is a scroll inscribed '*CARABINIERS*'. The badge is in gilding metal.

The regiment traced its origins back to the Napoleonic Wars but did not adopt the above title until 1884. The Hampshire Rose reflects the regiment's county of origin and the crossed carbines its original role.

Converted to artillery in 1920, the regiment amalgamated with the Hampshire Royal Horse Artillery to form a two-battery brigade, the 95th (Hampshire Yeomanry) Brigade RA. In 1939, the regiment was converted to an anti-aircraft regiment and mobilised as the 72nd Anti-Aircraft Regiment RA. One battery of the new regiment, 217th Heavy Anti-Aircraft Battery, was designated the Hampshire Carabiniers and continued to wear the above badge.

Initially serving in the United Kingdom, it landed with the First Army in North Africa in November 1942 and later served in Italy.

THE QUEEN'S OWN DORSET YEOMANRY

served as
94th (Hants and Dorset) Field Regiment RA
141st (Queen's Own Dorset Yeomanry) Field Regiment RA

The Garter ensigned by an Imperial Crown. Within the Garter the word *'DORSET'* inscribed on a scroll. Above the scroll but still within the Garter, the initials *'QO'* and below the scroll the initial *'Y'* and the whole within a laurel wreath. On the wreath are scrolls inscribed *'SOUTH AFRICA 1900–1901'* and across the base of the wreath, a further scroll inscribed *'THE GREAT WAR'*. The badge is found in both white metal and bronze.

Badge backing. A rectangular patch of dark green was worn behind the badge. Dark green had been the regimental colour since the regiment was formed in 1794 and had been worn behind the badge since 1920 to commemorate the actions which the Dorset Yeomanry had fought in the Great War, notably at Gallipoli and in the Palestine Campaign.

Initially raised during the Napoleonic Wars and disbanded at their conclusion, the Dorset Yeomanry was re-embodied in 1830 at the time of civil unrest in the county and had been in continuous existence until the post-Second World War amalgamations. It was given the title the Queen's Own in 1843, but the above badge dates only from 1920.

As part of the Imperial Yeomanry, the Queen's Own Dorset Yeomanry served in the Second Boer War for which it was awarded its first battle honour: 'South Africa'. It also served with distinction in the First World War and it was to include its two battle honours that the badge was re-designed in 1920.

Immediately after the Great War, the Dorset Yeomanry became one of the first yeomanry regiments to be converted to artillery, being amalgamated with the West Somerset Yeomanry to form the 94th (Dorset and Somerset)

Brigade RA. In 1929, the Brigade was re-organised to become an entirely Dorset-based formation and its title changed to the 94th (Queen's Own Dorset Yeomanry) Brigade RA.

In 1938 its title was again changed to the 94th (Queen's Own Dorset Yeomanry) Field Regiment RA, and a duplicate regiment, the 141st Field Regiment, was raised in the following year. It might have been supposed that the 94th Field Regiment, as the senior of the two formations, would have continued to bear the title of the Dorset Yeomanry. However, owing to an administrative misunderstanding, the 94th had its title changed to the 94th (Hants and Dorset) Field Regiment and adopted the cap-badge and other insignia of the Royal Artillery. It was left to the junior regiment, the 141st (Queen's Own Dorset Yeomanry) Field Regiment to continue to wear the QODY badge.

While the 94th Field Regiment, as part of 43rd (Wessex) Division, played a leading role in the North West Europe Campaign, including the Rhine Crossing, the 141st Field Regiment remained in England throughout the war.

THE HERTFORDSHIRE YEOMANRY

served as
79th (Herts Yeomanry) Heavy Anti-Aircraft Regiment RA
86th (Herts Yeomanry) Field Regiment RA
135th (Herts Yeomanry) Field Regiment RA
191st (Herts Yeomanry) Field Regiment RA

A hart trippant in water. The badge is in gilding metal.

The Hertfordshire Yeomanry was formed in 1871 when the South Hertfordshire Yeomanry and the remaining troop of the North Hertfordshire Yeomanry combined. The new regiment adopted the above badge which was taken from the arms of the county.

In 1920 the Hertfordshire Yeomanry converted to artillery as part of the 86th (East Anglian (Herts Yeomanry)) Brigade RFA, but in 1938 was re-designated as the 86th (Herts Yeomanry) Field Regiment RA. In the same year another artillery regiment, the 79th (Herts Yeomanry) Heavy Anti-Aircraft Regiment was formed. The continued expansion of the Territorial Army in the period immediately preceding the Second World War saw a duplicate of the 86th, the 135th Field Regiment, being raised. Shortly afterwards, a fourth regiment, the 191st (Herts Yeomanry) Field Regiment, was formed from units of 86th and 135th.

However, the above cap-badge appears only to have been worn by the 86th and 79th Regiments. The 135th Field Regiment, which was lost at Singapore, and the 191st Field Regiment both wore Royal Artillery insignia from their formation.

Even so, neither the 86th nor the 79th wore the badge throughout the war. The 79th wore the Hertfordshire Yeomanry badge while serving with the BEF in 1939–40, but adopted the Royal Artillery badge after the withdrawal from Dunkirk. Conversely, the 86th Field Regiment adopted the Royal Artillery badge on mobilisation in 1939, but when it was subsequently equipped with self-propelled guns prior to the Normandy landings, the regiment opted for the black beret of the Royal Armoured Corps and replaced its artillery badge with that of the Hertfordshire Yeomanry.

THE BERKSHIRE YEOMANRY

served as
145th (Berkshire Yeomanry) Field Regiment RA

The White Horse of Berkshire above a scroll inscribed 'BERKSHIRE'. The badge is in gilding metal.

Badge backing. A rectangular black patch was worn behind the badge.

The first Troops of Yeomanry were raised in Berkshire in 1794 and in 1803 they were formed into the 1st Berkshire Regiment of Yeomanry Cavalry. In 1853 its title was changed to the Royal Berkshire Yeomanry Cavalry, but on the formation of the Territorial Force in 1908, the regiment's title was again changed becoming simply the Berkshire Yeomanry.

The regiment was based at Hungerford and up to 1902 had the star and crescent from that borough's coat of arms as its badge. In 1902, the regiment adopted a representation of the White Horse of Uffingham as a symbol being more representative of the county as a whole.

After distinguished service in the Great War, in which a member of the regiment gained the first yeomanry VC, the Berkshire Yeomanry was converted to artillery in 1920 when it provided two batteries in the 99th (Bucks and Berks Yeomanry) Brigade RA. This new unit adopted Royal Artillery badges from its formation and when, on the expansion of the Territorial Army in 1939, the two Berkshire batteries were expanded to form a duplicate regiment, the 145th (Berkshire Yeomanry) Field Regiment, that, too, wore artillery insignia.

The regiment continued to wear RA badges until the end of 1944 when it was preparing to embark for the Far East. The White Horse badge was then re-introduced and, except when worn with the Field Service cap, it was worn with a black rectangular backing.

THE ROYAL DEVON YEOMANRY ARTILLERY

served as
96th (Royal Devon Yeomanry Artillery) Field Regiment RA
142nd (Royal Devon Yeomanry Artillery) Field Regiment RA

The crest of Lord Rolle within a circlet inscribed '*ROYAL DEVON YEOMANRY ARTILLERY*' surmounted by the Royal Crest. The badge is generally in gilding metal although examples are found in white metal.

The main device of the badge was the crest of Lord Rolle of Stevenstone who, during the French Revolutionary Wars, raised and commanded two regiments from which the Royal Devon Yeomanry Artillery was ultimately formed. In 1920 the two regiments, the 1st North Devon Yeomanry (raised in 1801) and the Royal North Devon Yeomanry (raised in 1803) were amalgamated to form the 96th (Devonshire Yeomanry) Brigade RA, but in 1923 its title was changed to the Royal Devon Yeomanry Artillery. Following the change of title, the above badge was approved in December 1924, the regiment being the only unit to avail itself of the War Office option to acquire a new badge on its change of role to artillery.

The regiment's name was again changed in 1938 when it became the 96th (Royal Devon Yeomanry Artillery) Field Regiment. The following year a duplicate regiment, the 142nd (Royal Devon Yeomanry Artillery) Field Regiment was raised and it, too, wore the above badge.

During the Second World War, the 96th Field Regiment remained in the United Kingdom until 1945 when it was posted to the Far East and saw service in Burma. The 142nd was the first artillery regiment to be involved in the invasion of Europe, being among the first troops ashore at Salerno in 1943. The regiment subsequently fought in the Italian Campaign until the end of the war in Europe.

THE DUKE OF YORK'S OWN LOYAL SUFFOLK HUSSARS

served as

55th (Suffolk Hussars) Anti-Tank Regiment RA

A castle with a flag on each of two towers facing left. Below the castle, the date '1793' and a scroll below the date inscribed 'LOYAL SUFFOLK HUSSARS'. The castle and date are in gilding metal and the scroll is in white metal.

The Loyal Suffolk Hussars was raised in 1793 at the outset of the Napoleonic Wars and took for its badge a representation of the castle at Bury St Edmunds where the regimental headquarters were situated. The secondary title of the Duke of York's Own was granted to the regiment in 1892 to commemorate the fact that the then Duke of York (later King George V) had been appointed Honorary Colonel.

In 1920, in common with many other yeomanry regiments, the Loyal Suffolk Hussars was converted to artillery, forming, with the Norfolk Yeomanry, the 108th (Suffolk and Norfolk Yeomanry) Brigade RFA. Two batteries were raised in each county and, somewhat unusually, their personnel continued to wear the badges of their respective regiments.

At the time of the Munich Crisis in 1938, there was a change of role and the 108th Brigade became the 55th (Suffolk and Norfolk Yeomanry) Anti-Tank Regiment. In 1939 the regiment divided: the Suffolk Hussars, as the senior regiment remained as the 55th, while the Norfolk batteries expanded to form the 65th (Norfolk Yeomanry) Anti-Tank Regiment.

On the outbreak of war, the 55th Regiment was incorporated into the 5th (East Anglian) Division, but it was subsequently transferred to the 9th (West Riding) Division with which formation it went to Normandy in 1944.

THE QUEEN'S OWN WORCESTERSHIRE HUSSARS

served as

53rd (Queen's Own Worcestershire Hussars) Anti-Tank Regiment RA

Within a laurel wreath surmounted by an Imperial Crown, a sprig of pear blossom. Superimposed on the wreath, a scroll inscribed '*QUEEN'S OWN WORCESTERSHIRE HUSSARS*'. The pear blossom is in white metal and the remainder of the badge is in gilding metal.

The regiment was originally raised during the Napoleonic Wars but the above title dates from 1837 following a visit by Queen Victoria to Whitley Court in Worcestershire when the regiment formed the guard of honour. The sprig of pear blossom in the badge was traditionally associated with Worcestershire, representing, as it did, one of the county's major industries. However, it was not adopted as the regiment's badge until 1899 and the bi-metal version was not introduced until 1913.

Transferred to the Royal Artillery in 1920, the Worcestershire Hussars combined with the Oxfordshire Hussars to form the 100th (Worcestershire and Oxfordshire Yeomanry) Field Brigade but, even so, the batteries formed from the Worcestershire Hussars kept their own badge. In 1938, the unit changed roles becoming the 53rd Anti-Tank Regiment. On the expansion of the Territorial Army in 1939, the two yeomanry regiments separated, with the Worcestershire Hussars, as the senior regiment, remaining as the 53rd. While on separation the Oxfordshire Hussars adopted Royal Artillery insignia, the Worcestershire Hussars kept its pear blossom badge.

As an anti-tank regiment in the 48th Division it was the first TA regiment to go abroad in the Second World War. In 1943 it became an airborne artillery regiment as the 53rd (Queen's Own Worcestershire Hussars) Air Landing Light Regiment RA. In that role it returned to France with the 6th Airborne Division on D-Day and it subsequently took part in the Rhine Crossing.

THE QUEEN'S OWN ROYAL GLASGOW YEOMANRY

served as

54th (Queen's Own Royal Glasgow Yeomanry) Anti-Tank Regiment RA
64th (Queen's Own Royal Glasgow Yeomanry) Anti-Tank Regiment RA

Two badges were worn:

left. The Crest of Scotland over sprays of thistles. The badge is in gilding metal.

right. A circular strap inscribed 'QUEEN'S OWN ROYAL GLASGOW YEOMANRY' surmounted by the Royal Crest. In the centre of the strap, the lion from the Crest of Scotland. The badge is in gilding metal.

The Queen's Own Glasgow Yeomanry was raised in 1848, although troops of yeomanry had existed in Glasgow previously. Its original title was the Queen's Own Royal Glasgow and Lower Ward of Lanarkshire Yeomanry, a title which it retained until 1914. The regiment had been granted its royal title to mark the visit of Queen Victoria to Glasgow in 1848 when the regiment had provided the mounted escort.

The main device on both badges was the Royal Crest of Scotland, reflecting the royal title of the regiment. The smaller badge was originally the regiment's collar-badge, but was later worn as a cap-badge in the beret.

In 1920, the Glasgow Yeomanry converted to artillery to form the 101st (Queen's Own Glasgow Yeomanry) Brigade RFA, but in 1939 came a change of role and a change in title; the regiment becoming the 54th (QORGY) Anti-Tank Regiment. In the same year a duplicate regiment, the 64th, also with an anti-tank role, was formed.

The 54th Anti-Tank Regiment served briefly in France with the BEF in 1940 and returned to North West Europe in 1944. The 64th saw active service in the Western Desert, Sicily and Italy.

THE SURREY YEOMANRY (QUEEN MARY'S REGIMENT)

served as
98th (Surrey Yeomanry) Field Regiment RA

Within the Garter surmounted by an Imperial Crown, the cypher of the late Queen Mary. Below is a scroll inscribed '*QUEEN MARY'S REGIMENT SURREY YEOMANRY*'. The badge is found in either white metal or gilding metal.

Founded in 1901 as the Surrey Imperial Yeomanry, the regiment was granted its current title and badge on the coronation of King George V. The main device of the badge is the cypher of Queen Mary, from whom the regiment took its secondary title.

The Surrey Yeomanry was converted to artillery in 1933, providing two batteries of the 98th (Surrey and Sussex Yeomanry) Brigade RFA and although forming a joint unit, personnel of each respective regiment continued to wear their own badges. In 1939 the two regiments regained their separate identities, the Surrey Yeomanry forming the 98th (Surrey Yeomanry) Field Regiment , while the Sussex batteries were expanded into a similar field regiment.

The 98th Field Regiment fought in France as part of the BEF and after withdrawal from Europe went to the Western Desert to join the Eighth Army. It took part in the Battle of El Alamein and subsequently, after being equipped with SP guns, fought in the Italian Campaign where it was heavily involved in the Battle of Monte Cassino.

THE NORFOLK YEOMANRY
(THE KING'S OWN ROYAL REGIMENT)

served as
65th (Norfolk Yeomanry) Anti-Tank Regiment RA

The Royal Cypher of King George VI ensigned with an Imperial Crown. The badge is in gilding metal.

Badge backing. A 2-inch square yellow patch was worn behind the badge in the GS cap for a short time in 1943. The choice of the backing had no historical significance, but in the words of Colonel Boag, who served in the regiment: 'We took it on ourselves to be different – but it only lasted six months before being told to remove it.'

The Norfolk Yeomanry had a somewhat chequered career in respect of the titles which it has borne. The first regiment, the Norfolk Rangers, raised in 1782, was one of the earliest yeomanry formations and the Napoleonic Wars resulted in the raising of two more yeomanry regiments in the county. Although they had all been disbanded by 1828, one regiment was re-formed in 1831 to meet a possible threat of civil disorder and was later given the title of Prince Albert's Own Norfolk Yeomanry. This was stood down in 1848 to be replaced in 1862 by the Norwich Light Horse Volunteers which, in turn, was disbanded in 1867.

The Second Boer War in 1899–1902 brought about a revival of the regiment as the King's Own Norfolk Yeomanry, but that title was changed in 1906 to the one shown above. It is because of the regiment's close association with the sovereign that the badge consists solely of the Royal Cypher.

After service in the Great War as an infantry battalion, the regiment combined with the Loyal Suffolk Hussars to form the 108th (Suffolk and Norfolk Yeomanry) Field Brigade RA in 1922.

On the expansion of the Territorial Army in 1939, the Norfolk Yeomanry resumed its own identity, although still remaining in an artillery role. It became the 65th (Norfolk Yeomanry) Anti-Tank Regiment but continued to wear the above badge.

The regiment initially served with 50th (Northumbrian) Division in the BEF and after the evacuation from Dunkirk was sent to the Western Desert. It was later transferred to the 7th Armoured Division with which it saw further service in North Africa and Italy. However, in 1943, together with the remainder of the division, it was withdrawn from Italy to prepare for Operation Overlord and ended the war in North West Europe.

THE SUSSEX YEOMANRY

served as
144th (Sussex Yeomanry) Field Regiment RA

On a shield six martlets, the whole on an ornamental ground surmounted by an Imperial Crown. Below the shield is a scroll inscribed 'SUSSEX YEOMANRY'. The badge is in gilding metal.

The regiment was formed from the Sussex Imperial Yeomanry which was raised in 1901 for service in South Africa. However, the badge was only adopted in 1906 and the title of the regiment not amended until the formation of the Territorial Force in 1908.

The main device of the badge was a shield with six martlets, taken from the coat of arms of the county.

In 1922, the Sussex Yeomanry was united with the Surrey Yeomanry in the 98th (Surrey and Sussex) Brigade RFA, with each regiment providing two batteries. In common with a number of artillery units composed of two yeomanry regiments, the personnel of each were allowed to retain their own badges. In 1939, the two Sussex batteries were expanded to form a duplicate artillery regiment – 144th Field Regiment – which incorporated Sussex Yeomanry into its title.

The 144th Field Regiment served in the United Kingdom until 1940, after which it was moved to the Middle East, seeing service in Egypt, Iraq, Persia and Palestine.

THE CITY OF LONDON YEOMANRY
(THE ROUGH RIDERS)

served as
11th (City of London Yeomanry (Rough Riders)) Light Anti-Aircraft
Regiment RA

Two badges were worn:

a. The Royal Artillery (*qv*)

b. A spur with a rowel to the right entwined with the letters 'RR'. The spur is in white metal and the letters are in gilding metal.

The Rough Riders was raised in 1899 for service in South Africa as the 20th Battalion of Imperial Yeomanry, taking its name from that of Colonel Theodore Roosevelt's volunteer cavalry, which had fought in Cuba during the Spanish-American War the previous year. The badge of a spur alluded to the regiment's cavalry origins.

After their return from the Boer War in 1901, members of the regiment formed the 1st County of London Imperial Yeomanry (Rough Riders). However, on the establishment of the Territorial Force in 1908, the regiment was re-designated as the City of London Yeomanry, although it retained its secondary title of the Rough Riders.

In 1920, the City of London Yeomanry was converted to artillery, forming a battery in the 11th (HAC and City of London Yeomanry) Brigade RHA and adopting Royal Artillery cap-badges. With the expansion of the Territorial Army in 1939, the Rough Riders regained its identity, becoming the 11th (City of London Yeomanry) Light Anti-Aircraft Regiment. Although the new regiment retained Royal Artillery insignia, on the introduction of the FS cap, it adopted its former yeomanry collar-badge for use as a cap-badge.

THE ESSEX YEOMANRY

served as
104th (Essex Yeomanry) Regiment RHA
147th (Essex Yeomanry) Field Regiment RA

Two badges were worn:

left. A circlet inscribed '*DECUS ET TUTAMEN*' (Honour and Protection) ensigned by an Imperial Crown. In the centre is a shield bearing three seaxes. The badge is in gilding metal.

right. A circlet inscribed '*ESSEX YEOMANRY*' ensigned by an Imperial Crown. In the centre of the circlet is a shield bearing three seaxes. Below the circlet is a scroll inscribed '*DECUS ET TUTAMEN*'. The badge is in gilding metal.

The Essex Yeomanry had its origins, as so many other yeomanry regiments, in the troops of yeomanry raised at the time of the Napoleonic Wars. However, none of the Essex units had a continuous existence and the Essex Yeomanry was not formed until 1908. Its immediate antecedent was the Essex Imperial Yeomanry which itself was not raised until after the South African War of 1899–1902 when it was formed out of the Essex Troop of the Loyal Suffolk Hussars.

The shield with three seaxes, which was common to both badges, was taken from the Essex county coat of arms, while the motto, '*Decus et Tutamen*', was taken from the badge of an earlier formation, the West Essex Yeomanry.

The first of the badges was introduced when the regiment was incorporated into the Territorial Force in 1908. The second was introduced in 1916 and from then until the outbreak of the Second World War, the first badge continued only as a collar-badge. With the introduction of the Field Service cap and, later, the beret, the first badge was again used as a cap-badge.

After service in France and Flanders in the Great War, the regiment was converted to artillery in 1921 as the 104th (Essex Yeomanry) Brigade, Royal

Horse Artillery. In 1932 the Brigade was augmented when it was joined by the Essex RFA which provided 339 Battery. The regiment's title was changed in 1939 to the 104th (Essex Yeomanry) Regiment RHA and at the same time, on the doubling of the Territorial Army, a second regiment, the 147th (Essex Yeomanry) Field Regiment RA, was raised.

Both regiments wore the above badge.

104th (Essex Yeomanry) Regiment went to the Middle East in 1940 and took part in the North Africa and Italian campaigns, ending the war in Austria. During 1942, 414th Battery was detached from the regiment and sent to Burma to strengthen the forces retreating from Rangoon. It was then expanded to form 14th Regiment RHA and ceased to wear the Essex Yeomanry badge.

The 147th (Essex Yeomanry) Field Regiment, after landing in Normandy in June 1944 and fighting through the Low Countries, was disbanded in December 1944 when its personnel were dispersed to provide infantry reinforcements.

THE SCOTTISH HORSE

served as
79th (Scottish Horse) Medium Regiment RA
80th (Scottish Horse) Medium Regiment RA

An oval inscribed 'SCOTTISH HORSE 1900' and enclosed by a wreath of juniper and bay and ensigned with a Scottish crown. Superimposed on the oval is a St Andrew's Cross and below is a scroll inscribed 'SOUTH AFRICA'. Below that is a second scroll inscribed '1900, 1901, 1902'. The badge is found in gilding metal and white metal.

The Scottish Horse was raised by the Duke of Atholl for service in South Africa in 1900, and although a troop of Yeomanry Cavalry had been raised in Perthshire in the early nineteenth century there was no linear connection between the two units.

The badge of the Scottish Horse is unique in that it is the only one in the British Army to display a Scottish crown. The wreath of bay leaves and juniper was taken from the badge of the Clan Murray of which the Duke of Atholl was chief. The battle honour displayed on the badge was gained in the Second Boer War.

After dismounted service in the First World War, the regiment became a horsed cavalry unit again in 1920 and remained so until 1939 when it was converted to artillery, forming the 79th and 80th (Scottish Horse) Medium Regiments RA.

The 80th served in the Western Desert with the 51st (Highland) Division, later moving to Sicily and Italy. The 79th Medium Regiment landed in Normandy in June 1944 and saw service in North West Europe until the collapse of Germany.

THE WEST YORKSHIRE REGIMENT
8th (Leeds Rifles) Battalion TA

served as
96th (Leeds Rifles) Heavy Anti-Aircraft Regiment RA

A cross, similar to the cross of the Order of the Bath, surmounted by an Imperial Crown. On the arms of the cross the following battle-honours are inscribed: (top) *'NAMUR 1695'*, *'TOURNAY'*, *'CORUNNA'*, *'JAVA'*, *'WATERLOO'*; (left) *'SOUTH AFRICA 1899–02'*, *'ARMENTIERES 1914'*, *'NEUVE CHAPPELLE'*, *'SOMME 1916, 1918'*, *'YPRES 1917, 1918'*; (right) *'CAMBRAI 1917, 1918'*, *'VILLERS BRETONNEUX'*, *'LYS'*, *'PIAVE'*, *'SUVLA'*; (bottom) *'BHUTOORE'*, *'SEVASTAPOL'*, *'NEW ZEALAND'*, *'AFGHANISTAN'*, *'RELIEF OF LADYSMITH'*. Below the cross, a scroll inscribed *TARDENOIS*. In the centre of the cross, a circlet inscribed *'LEEDS RIFLES'* and within this, a bugle-horn with strings surmounted by an Imperial Crown. The whole is surrounded by a laurel wreath. On the left branch of the wreath is a scroll inscribed *'7TH 8TH BNS'* and on the right a scroll inscribed *'PWO'*. Across the base of the wreath, a further scroll inscribed *'WEST YORKSHIRE REGT'*. The badge is found both in white and blackened metal.

The badge of the Leeds Rifles, in common with those of many of the units which claim descent from the mid-nineteenth century Rifle Volunteers, is based on the cross of the Order of the Bath, with a strung bugle in the centre of the cross. Where this badge differs was in the battle-honours which it bore, for instead of carrying only its own battle-honour, Tardenois, the badge of the Leeds Rifles also carried those of its parent regiment, the West Yorkshire Regiment. When the Territorial Force was established in 1908, Volunteer

Battalions were expressly prevented from carrying battle-honours awarded to their parent regiments and it is uncertain how the Leeds Rifles was able to contravene this regulation.

The 8th Battalion of the West Yorkshire Regiment was originally raised as the 4th Battalion of the West Yorkshire Militia with the title of 'The Leeds Regiment' in 1853 and re-mustered as one of four battalions of the West Yorkshire Rifle Volunteers in 1859. Following a number of changes of title, the Volunteer battalions were incorporated into the Territorial component of the West Yorkshire Regiment in 1908 with both the 7th and 8th Battalions having the additional title of 'The Leeds Rifles'.

Although the official function of the Territorial Force battalions was home defence, most of the personnel in all the Territorial battalions of the West Yorkshire Regiment volunteered for overseas service on the outbreak of the First World War. The two Leeds Rifles battalions went to France in April 1915, the 8th being divided into the 1/8th and 2/8th Battalions. Because of casualties, the two battalions were amalgamated in February 1918, but the new formation still kept the title of the Leeds Rifles. The battalion fought on the Somme and at Passchendaele, but the battle-honour Tardenois dates from July 1918 when the Leeds Rifles received the Croix de Guerre from the French Government for the taking of Mont de Bligny in the Battle of Tardenois.

After the Great War, the 7th and 8th Battalions were united and the above cap-badge, incorporating the battle-honour of the 8th, was adopted. The amalgamated battalion was converted to artillery in 1936, as the 96th (Leeds Rifles) Anti-Aircraft Brigade RA. In 1938, however, the battalion was divided into its original components, with the 7th Battalion becoming the 45th Battalion, the Royal Tank Corps and adopting the RTC (and later, the Royal Tank Regiment) cap-badge. The 8th Battalion remained in an artillery role, but its designation changed to the 96th (Leeds Rifles) Heavy Anti-Aircraft Regiment.

Despite the change of role and title, the regiment continued to wear its Leeds Rifles cap-badge.

THE HAMPSHIRE REGIMENT
8th (Princess Beatrice's Isle of Wight Rifles) Battalion TA

served as
530th Coast Regiment (Princess Beatrice's Isle of Wight Rifles) RA

A representation of Carisbrooke Castle within a circlet inscribed *'ISLE OF WIGHT RIFLES'* within a laurel wreath; above the circlet a scroll inscribed *'SOUTH AFRICA 1900–01'* and below the circlet another scroll inscribed *'PRINCESS BEATRICE'S'*. The whole is ensigned with an Imperial Crown. The badge is in blackened metal.

The central device of the badge, Carisbrooke Castle, was originally adopted by the Isle of Wight Volunteers raised at the time of the French Revolutionary Wars. Although the unit was disbanded after the defeat of Napoleon in 1815, the representation of the castle was again used in the badge of the Isle of Wight Volunteers raised in 1859. Like its predecessor, this regiment was also raised to combat the threat of a French invasion, this time by Napoleon III. Although many of the volunteer regiments raised at this time claimed to be rifle units and adopted the dark green of the Rifle regiments, in the case of the Isle of Wight Volunteers, this association was reinforced by the fact that its first two adjutants and its second commanding officer were all drawn from the Rifle Brigade.

In 1880 the unit became the 1st Isle of Wight Rifle Volunteer Corps and five years later it was incorporated into the Hampshire Regiment as the 5th (Isle of Wight, Princess Beatrice's) Volunteer Battalion. Princess Beatrice, the youngest daughter of Queen Victoria, was the wife of Prince Henry of Battenburg who had been Governor of the Isle of Wight and of Carisbrooke Castle, and it was through her husband that she had a close association with the battalion.

The battalion changed its name again in 1908 when it became the 8th (Princess Beatrice's Isle of Wight Rifles) Battalion, the Hampshire Regiment, on which date the above badge was adopted. The battalion saw distinguished service in the Great War at Gallipoli and Palestine, but immediately after the war there was a proposal to change its role to that of an artillery regiment.

Strong local opposition to the change, supported by Princess Beatrice, succeeded in having the proposal quashed. However, it was only a temporary respite, for in 1937, ironically the year in which Princess Beatrice accepted the Honorary Colonelcy of the battalion, it was formally transferred to the Royal Artillery as Prince Beatrice's (Isle of Wight Rifles) Heavy Brigade RA. Another change of title followed in 1938, the unit becoming the 530th Coast Regiment (Princess Beatrice's Isle of Wight Rifles) RA.

Despite the change of role and of titles, the regiment was permitted to retain the original battalion cap-badge and black buttons. In addition, the regiment was allowed to continue to wear its black and green ceremonial dress – the latter earning it the nickname 'The Green Gunners' – the only unit in the Royal Artillery to have that distinction.

During the Second World War the regiment manned the forts around the island, although drafts from the regiment served in theatres of war as far apart as Iceland and Imphal. At one stage in 1940, the regiment was so depleted by such postings that some of its guns were manned by tailors' dummies to confuse German aircrew.

THE SHERWOOD FORESTERS
7th (The Robin Hoods) Battalion TA

served as
42nd (Robin Hoods, The Sherwood Foresters) Searchlight Regiment RA

A cross, as in the cross of the Order of the Bath, thereon a circlet inscribed '*THE ROBIN HOODS*' enclosing a strung bugle surmounted by an Imperial Crown. The cross in enclosed in a laurel wreath and surmounted by an Imperial Crown. The battle honour, South Africa, is on three arms of the cross, viz: '*SOUTH*', on the left, '*AFRICA*' on the right and '*1900–02*' on the bottom arm. The badge is in white metal.

The badge was based on that of the Rifle Brigade, as was that of many of the rifle volunteer units raised in the mid-nineteenth century, while the battle honour displayed on the wreath was gained by the regiment in the Second Boer War.

The regiment was formed in 1859, along with numerous other rifle volunteer units, to meet the threatened French invasion and after several changes of title became, in 1881, the 1st Nottinghamshire (Robin Hood) Rifle Volunteer Corps. On the formation of the Territorial Force in 1908, the Robin Hoods became part of the corps of the Sherwood Foresters, becoming the 7th (Robin Hoods) Battalion of that regiment. It was then that the above badge was adopted.

After serving as infantry during the Great War, the battalion underwent a change of role in December 1936, becoming the 42nd (Robin Hoods, The Sherwood Foresters) Anti-Aircraft Battalion RE. Four years later all anti-aircraft units were transferred to the Royal Artillery and the battalion became the 42nd (Robin Hoods, The Sherwood Foresters) Searchlight Regiment RA.

Initially the battalion had worn a blackened badge, as had most of the units which traced their lineage back to the rifle volunteers, but on conversion to an anti-aircraft role, it adopted the badge of the Royal Engineers. However, on transfer to the Royal Artillery in 1940, the then Commanding Officer, Lieutenant Colonel Coley, was able to persuade the War Office that the Robin Hoods be permitted to revert to its original cap-badge which the unit then wore for the rest of the war.

The only difference between the new badge and the old was that the latter version was produced in white metal.

The Robin Hoods took part in the North West Europe Campaign of 1944–45 and for its distinguished service in Belgium it was awarded the Croix de Guerre, a replica of the ribbon of which was subsequently worn below the regimental shoulder title.

20TH COUNTY OF LONDON REGIMENT (THE QUEEN'S OWN)

served as
34th (The Queen's Own West Kent) Searchlight Regiment RA

The White Horse of Kent standing upon a scroll inscribed in Old English *'INVICTA'* (Unconquered). Below this is a second scroll inscribed *'20TH BATT THE LONDON REGT'*. The badge is white metal.

The main device of the badge was the White Horse of Kent, taken from the arms of the county of Kent and with which the regiment had always been associated.

The history of the regiment can be traced back to the Greenwich Volunteer unit which fought in the English Civil War and was present at the Battle of Newbury in 1643. However, its direct antecedent was the Rifle Volunteer Corps raised in 1859 to combat a possible invasion by the French.

Following the changes in the organisation of the army brought about by the Cardwell Reforms of 1882, the Rifle Volunteers in West Kent were grouped into two battalions, the 2nd and 3rd Volunteer Battalions, of the Queen's Own (Royal West Kent Regiment). On the formation of the Territorial Force in 1908, the two battalions were amalgamated and the unit thus formed became the 20th (County of London) Battalion, The London Regiment – a regiment which was composed entirely of Territorial battalions.

Although the 20th Battalion did not, like some of the other units in the London Regiment, retain the name of its parent regiment, it was authorised to continue to wear the Royal West Kent Regiment cap-badge and buttons and to retain the black facings of the 2nd Volunteer Battalion, the only change to the cap-badge being the addition of the second scroll.

100

In 1922, with a change in component formations of the London regiment, the title of the 20th Battalion was changed to the 20th London Regiment (The Queen's Own), although there was no change made to the badge.

In 1935, the battalion was converted from an infantry to an anti-aircraft role, but although it became part of the Corps of Royal Engineers, which initially was responsible for search-light units, it was allowed to retain its cap-badge and Colours. In this role, its first title still referred to the battalion as being part of the London Regiment, but this was changed in 1936, when it became the 34th (The Queen's Own Royal West Kent) Anti-Aircraft Battalion, Royal Engineers. In 1937, a fourth company, No 302 Company RE, was incorporated into the battalion but this unit retained its Royal Engineers' cap-badge and other insignia.

When in 1940, the Royal Artillery took over all searchlight units, the Queen's Own became the 34th (Queen's Own Royal West Kent) Searchlight Regiment RA, which it remained until January 1945. While the three batteries which had originated as the 20th London Regiment continued to wear the West Kent badge, 302 Company became 302 Battery and changed to Royal Artillery badges.

The regiment not only took part in the Battle of Britain, during which it destroyed seven enemy aircraft by small arms fire, but remained deployed in Kent and Sussex in aid of RAF night-fighters until 1944. The regiment was disbanded in January 1945, the bulk of its personnel being transferred to the 633rd Garrison Regiment RA, which itself was placed in suspended animation in the October of that year.

THE SOUTH WALES BORDERERS
1st Bn The Monmouthshire Regiment

served as
68th (Monmouthshire) Searchlight Regiment RA

A laurel wreath surmounted by an Imperial Crown. On the wreath are battle honour scrolls inscribed as follows: (left) 'SOUTH AFRICA 1900–02', 'YPRES 1915, 1918', 'SOMME 1916', 'SCARPE 1917', 'CAMBRAI 1917', 1918'; (right) 'ST JULIAN', 'ARRAS 1917', 'LANGERMAROCK 1917', 'HINDENBURG LINE', 'ADEN'. In the centre of the wreath, a Welsh Dragon standing on ground. Across the base of the wreath, a scroll inscribed 'FRANCE AND FLANDERS 1914–18'. The badge is in gilding metal.

Badge backing. When the badge was worn on the khaki cap GS or beret, it was worn with a square of 'Rifle' green backing.

The regiment originated in 1860 as the Monmouthshire Rifle Volunteer Corps but was subsequently incorporated into the South Wales Borderers as a Volunteer battalion at the time of the Cardwell Reforms. On the formation of the Territorial Force in 1908, it was re-designated the Monmouthshire Regiment – one of four units to be so honoured as Territorial regiments in their own right – although it remained part of the corps of the South Wales Borderers.

Between the two world wars, the regiment maintained three battalions and while the 2nd and 3rd Battalions retained the original 1908 badge of a Welsh Dragon on ground, the 1st Battalion adopted the above badge in 1925. This not only portrayed the Dragon, but gave due prominence to the distinguished service of the regiment in the First World War by recording its battle honours on the wreath – a practice usually adopted by Rifle regiments. It further sought to reinforce its Rifle origins by the adoption of a square of dark green behind the cap-badge.

While the 2nd and 3rd Battalions remained as infantry, the 1st Battalion was converted to an anti-aircraft role. It first became a searchlight regiment in 1938 as the 1st (Rifle) Bn, the Monmouthshire Regiment, (68th Searchlight Regiment), but its title was changed two years later when the Royal Artillery assumed control of all anti-aircraft units becoming the 68th (Monmouthshire Regiment) Searchlight Regiment RA.

The battalion changed its title and role twice more during the Second World War, finally becoming, in November 1944, the 609th Regiment RA (The Monmouthshire Regiment), but throughout these changes the above badge was worn.

OTHER INFANTRY BATTALIONS

which served with

THE ROYAL ARTILLERY

In addition to the battalions described earlier, over seventy former infantry battalions were converted to artillery regiments. Most of them adopted the Royal Artillery cap-badge and insignia, but the following battalions appear to have retained their original badges:

5th Bn	The Royal Northumberland Fusiliers
10th Bn	The Royal Fusiliers
5th Bn	The Lincolnshire Regiment
5th Bn	The Devonshire Regiment
7th Bn	The Devonshire Regiment
4th Bn	The Leicestershire Regiment
5th/8th Bn	The Cameronians (The Scottish Rifles)
1/6th Bn	The Essex Regiment
2/6th Bn	The Essex Regiment
7th Bn	The Essex Regiment
6th Bn	The Sherwood Foresters
9th Bn	The Middlesex Regiment
7th Bn	The Highland Light Infantry

Details of these badges appear in Section VI.

SECTION IV

OTHER ARMS

THE CORPS OF ROYAL ENGINEERS

Two badges were worn:

left. The Royal Cypher of King George VI within the Garter, the whole enclosed in a laurel wreath. Above, and resting upon the Garter between the ends of the wreath, an Imperial Crown. Below the Garter and resting upon the lower portion of the wreath, a scroll inscribed *'ROYAL ENGINEERS'*. The badge is in gilding metal.

right. A grenade with nine flames with, below, a scroll inscribed *'UBIQUE'* (Everywhere). The badge is in gilding metal or brass.

The original Corps of Royal Engineers was formed in 1716 but this had an all-officer establishment. A separate Corps of Soldier Artificers was created in 1772 in Gibraltar but after two changes of name, it amalgamated with the existing Corps of Royal Engineers in 1856.

The main device of the cap-badge, that of the Royal Cypher within the laurel wreath, was introduced in the reign of Queen Victoria, but the scroll below the Garter was not added until the accession of King Edward VII in 1902.

The grenade cap-badge, however, had much earlier antecedents, although it was not until 1922 that the present nine flame pattern was approved and adopted for all occasions. The second badge was officially only worn by officers, but the author has photographic evidence of the grenade badge being worn by Other Ranks in the dress Field Service cap. The badge was, presumably, a collar badge which had been mis-appropriated for use as a cap-badge and it is not known how widely this practice was adopted.

Although losing some of its functions to the Royal Corps of Signals in 1920 and to the Royal Electrical and Mechanical Engineers in 1942, the Royal Engineers served in every major operation in the Second World War.

The Corps of Royal Engineers
THE ROYAL MONMOUTHSHIRE
ROYAL ENGINEERS

Two badges were worn:

a. The badge of the Royal Engineers (*qv*)

b. The prince of Wales's coronet, plumes and motto '*ICH DIEN*' (I serve), surmounted by an Imperial Crown. On either side of the coronet the letters '*R*' and '*E*'. Below is a scroll inscribed '*ROYAL MONMOUTHSHIRE*'. The plume and motto are in white metal; the remainder of the badge is in gilding metal.

The Royal Monmouthshire Royal Engineers (Militia) was the senior regiment of the Territorial Army and took precedence immediately after the regular forces. It was, in fact, the last survivor of the Militia regiments which, in turn, could trace their origins back to the General Levies and Train Bands of medieval and Tudor times.

As the Monmouthshire and Brecon Militia, the regiment was given the prefix 'Royal' in 1793, changing its title in 1820 to the Royal Monmouthshire Militia. In 1877, following the Cardwell Reforms, it became part of the Corps of Royal Engineers and in 1896 it acquired the above title of the Royal Monmouthshire Royal Engineers, thus achieving the unique privilege of having two 'Royals' in its title.

At the beginning of the Second World War, the regiment wore the standard cap-badge of the Royal Engineers, but with RMRE shoulder-titles. The first recorded wearing of the second badge occurred on 23rd March 1944 when both companies of the regiment were inspected by King George VI, and in the words of the official history of the regiment:

The Regiment wore its own and present-day badge in their battle-dress caps on parade for the first time. The King commented favourably on the new cap-badge and said that he was very pleased to see the regiment wearing them, with the result that they have been worn ever since.

The cap-badge had been designed and produced by the late Colonel Everett in 1938 when he was adjutant of the regiment. He and his fellow officers seem to have worn it from that date, despite official regulations, although Senior NCOs and other ranks did not wear it until 1944, as indicated above.

In 1939, the Royal Monmouthshire Royal Engineers was mobilised and as 100 and 101 Field Companies RE went to France with the BEF, both companies fighting as infantry during the rearguard action of the Dunkirk withdrawal. The two companies returned to Normandy in 1944 and fought throughout the campaign in North West Europe, being among the first Sappers to cross the Seine and the Rhine.

THE ROYAL CORPS OF SIGNALS

An oval on which is inscribed '*ROYAL CORPS OF SIGNALS*' with, in the bottom centre, a terrestrial globe with a sprig of laurel on either side. The oval is surmounted by an Imperial Crown. In the centre of the oval is the figure of Mercury poised on his left foot on the globe. In his left hand he holds a caduceus and his right hand is held aloft. The oval and crown are in gilding metal, the remainder of the badge being in white metal.

The Royal Corps of Signals was formed from the Signal Service of the Royal Engineers in June 1920, being granted the prefix 'Royal' some six months later in recognition of the service performed in the Great War by its predecessor. The current badge was adopted at that date.

The main device on the badge is a representation of Mercury, who was the messenger of the Gods in Roman mythology, and who was usually depicted as carrying a caduceus or herald's wand. It was, therefore, appropriate that Mercury was chosen to represent the functions of the Royal Corps of Signals, while the fact that he is shown standing on a terrestrial globe signifies the world-wide role of the corps.

Units of the Royal Signals saw service in every single theatre of operations during the Second World War, being augmented by a number of regiments transferred from other arms. In addition to the 1st County of London Yeomanry (*qv*), which became a signals regiment as early as 1920, two other Yeomanry regiments were transferred to the Royal Corps of Signals in 1942: the North Somerset Yeomanry which became the 4th Air Formation Signals Regiment, and the Cheshire Yeomanry which became the 5th Line of Communications Signals Regiment.

Both these regiments, however, retained their own cap-badges.

The Royal Corps of Signals
1ST COUNTY OF LONDON YEOMANRY (MIDDLESEX, THE DUKE OF CAMBRIDGE'S HUSSARS)

served as
1st Cavalry Divisional Signals Regiment (Middlesex Yeomanry)
2nd Armoured Divisional Signals Regiment (Middlesex Yeomanry)

An eight-pointed star. In the centre, a circlet inscribed '*PRO ARIS ET FOCI*' (For our Hearths and Homes) '*MIDDLESEX YEOMANRY*'. Within the circlet is the Royal Cypher of King George VI. The badge is in white metal.

The Middlesex Yeomanry Cavalry was raised in 1838 and was granted the secondary title of the Duke of Cambridge's Hussars in 1884. After service as Imperial Yeomanry in South Africa it became, in 1908, the 1st County of London Yeomanry – a title which had formerly been held by the Rough Riders – and the above badge was adopted.

The main device of the badge, the cypher of the reigning monarch, was derived from the regiment's association with the Duke of Cambridge, one of Queen Victoria's sons, while the inscription on the circlet is one often found on yeomanry badges indicating, as it did, the prime function of yeomanry regiments.

In 1920 the regiment was re-constituted and became a divisional cavalry signals regiment. As the 1st Cavalry Divisional Signals Regiment (Middlesex Yeomanry), the regiment went to the Middle East in 1940 and saw service in Syria, Iraq and Crete. It was subsequently mechanised and served in North Africa. A duplicate regiment, the 2nd Armoured Divisional Signals Regiment (Middlesex Yeomanry), was raised in 1939 and also served in Greece and the Western Desert.

Despite being in the Royal Corps of Signals, both regiments wore the above badge.

THE ARMY AIR CORPS

An eagle facing right and resting on the uppermost of two bars carrying the letters '*AAC*', the whole within a laurel wreath surmounted by an Imperial Crown. The badge is in white metal.

The eagle on the badge symbolised the role of the corps – representing, as it does, aggression descending from the skies.

The Army Air Corps was formed in February 1942 and initially comprised the Glider Pilot Regiment and the Parachute Regiment. The latter obtained its own badge in May 1943 and the above badge was subsequently worn only by members of the Glider Pilot Regiment.

The Army Air Corps saw service in most theatres of war, but its major operations were in North West Europe where it enabled the Allied forces to gain their first foothold in Normandy and, later, across the Rhine.

The Army Air Corps
THE PARACHUTE REGIMENT

A pair of wings outspread horizontally upon which is an open parachute surmounted by the Royal Crest (a lion on the crown). The badge is in white metal.

Badge backing. The maroon beret signified the airborne forces and this in itself was sufficient backing. However, in addition the 15th (Scottish) Battalion wore a diamond patch of Hunting Stuart tartan behind its badge.

Formed in 1942, the Parachute Regiment originally wore the badge of the Army Air Corps, but in 1943 the above badge, which symbolises the role of the regiment, was adopted.

Sixteen battalions of the Parachute Regiment were raised during the Second World War. The 1st Battalion was originally No 2 Commando while the 2nd, 3rd and 4th Battalions were drawn from volunteers from all arms of the army. Seven subsequent battalions were formed from existing infantry units, although on conversion all adopted the above badge.

Like its parent corps, the Parachute Regiment saw active service in many theatres of war, but it was probably for its operations in North West Europe that it is most widely recognised.

SECTION V

THE FOOT GUARDS

THE GRENADIER GUARDS

A grenade fused proper. The badge is in gilding metal for ranks below that of sergeant. For sergeants the ball is embossed with the Royal Cypher and crown.

The Grenadier Guards is the senior infantry regiment in the British Army, having been raised from Royalist emigres by King Charles II while he was in exile in France. It was because of the loyalty of its personnel during the period of the Commonwealth that it was given the title of the First Regiment of Foot Guards in 1685. The regiment later distinguished itself at the Battle of Waterloo where it defeated the Grenadiers of Napoleon's Imperial Guard. As a result, it was created a regiment of Grenadiers and the current badge represents this title.

During the Second World War the regiment was increased from three to eight battalions, of which six saw active service.

All wore the above badge, even though three battalions were subsequently converted to armour.

THE COLDSTREAM GUARDS

The Star of the Order of the Garter. The badge is in gilding metal.

The regiment was formed in 1650 as a unit of the New Model Army of the Commonwealth. As was normal practice at the time, it took the name of its first commanding officer, General Monck, and as Monck's Regiment it was stationed for some time at Coldstream in the Scottish Borders, from where it marched south to assist in the Restoration of the monarchy. However, in 1661, following the Restoration, it was incorporated into the army of King Charles II and was created a Regiment of Foot Guards, taking its secondary title, by which it became known, from the town of Coldstream.

Although older than the Grenadier Guards, because of that regiment's Royalist connections, the Coldstream Guards took precedence after the Grenadiers.

Because of its close association with the sovereign, as part of the Brigade of Guards, the Coldstream Guards adopted the Star of the Order of the Garter as its cap-badge.

During the Second World War, in addition to the three Regular battalions, a further three battalions were raised. Battalions of the Coldstream Guards served with the BEF in 1939–40 and subsequently saw active service in North Africa, Italy and in the North West Europe Campaign.

THE SCOTS GUARDS

The Star of the Order of the Thistle. The badge is in gilding metal.

Like the Coldstream Guards, the Scots Guards, because of its association with the sovereign, based its badge on one of the Orders of Chivalry, in this case the Order of the Thistle, the senior Order of Chivalry in Scotland.

The Scots Guards was raised in 1660 following the Restoration of King Charles II and is thus the third senior regiment of Foot Guards. Initially known simply as the Third Foot Guards, the regiment subsequently became the Scots Fusilier Guards. In 1877 the current title was adopted and at the same time the present cap-badge introduced.

Six battalions of the regiment served in the Second World War, four of them seeing action in North Africa, Italy and North West Europe. In addition, elements of the Scots Guards served with No 1 (Guards) Parachute Pathfinder Company.

All units wore the above badge although the 3rd (Tank) Battalion wore it on the black beret invariably associated with armoured units.

THE IRISH GUARDS

The Star of the Order of St Patrick. The badge is in gilding metal.

The 4th Regiment of Foot Guards, the Irish Guards was formed in 1900 on the command of Queen Victoria to commemorate the bravery shown by Irish regiments in operations in the Second Boer War.

The badge, the Star of the Order of St Patrick, the Irish Order of Chivalry, was chosen to complement those of the Coldstream and Scots Guards which respectively wore badges representing English and Scottish Orders.

Three battalions of the Irish Guards served in the Second World War – the 1st and 3rd Battalions being incorporated in the Guards Armoured Division. All three battalions wore the above badge.

THE WELSH GUARDS

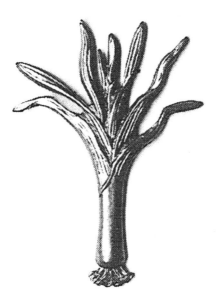

A Welsh leek. The badge is in gilding metal.

The Welsh Guards, the junior regiment of the Brigade of Guards, was not formed until 26 February 1915 when, at the express wish of King George V, a Welsh Regiment of Foot Guards was raised, the original recruits being largely drawn from Welshmen already serving in the Army. It was because of this influx of experienced officers and men that the Welsh Guards was in action within six months of the regiment's establishment.

During the Second World War, the Welsh Guards raised three war service and one training battalion in addition to the existing Regular battalions. All wore the above cap-badge.

SECTION VI

INFANTRY OF THE LINE

THE ROYAL SCOTS (THE ROYAL REGIMENT)

The Star of the Order of the Thistle. In the centre, St Andrew and Cross (voided) above a scroll inscribed '*THE ROYAL SCOTS*'. The centre and the scroll are in gilding metal and the star is in white metal. The piper's badge is all in white metal.

Badge backing. The 1st and Territorial Battalions wore a red insert behind the voided centre of the badge, while the 2nd Battalion wore a green insert. The badge itself was backed by a 3-inch square of Hunting Stuart tartan.

A warrant given by the Privy Council of Scotland under the authority of King Charles I embodied The Royal Scots in 1633 and, as a result, the regiment claimed pride of place as the senior infantry regiment of the line.

During the Second World War, The Royal Scots numbered four active service battalions and two holding battalions, but not all wore the above cap-badge.

In 1940, the 4th/5th Battalion (The Queen's Edinburghs) was transferred to the Royal Artillery after which it wore the RA cap-badge and other artillery insignia.

THE QUEEN'S ROYAL REGIMENT (WEST SURREY)

The Paschal Lamb. The badge is in gilding metal.

The senior English regiment of the line, the 2nd Foot, was raised in 1661 to garrison Tangier which had formed part of Catherine of Braganza's dowry on her marriage to King Charles II. It was through the regiment's association with Queen Catherine that it was accorded the title The Queen's Royal Regiment on its withdrawal to England on the evacuation of Tangier in 1685. The Paschal Lamb, the symbol of the House of Braganza, was confirmed as the badge of the regiment in 1751.

No fewer than sixteen battalions of The Queen's Royal Regiment served in the Second World War. In addition to the two Regular and two Territorial battalions, two battalions, the 6th and 7th, were transferred to the London Regiment in 1937 and they, together with the 5th, each raised a duplicate battalion.

The only battalion to be transferred to another arm was the 4th, which became first the 63rd Searchlight Regiment RA and later, in August 1940, the 127th Light Anti-Aircraft Regiment RA (Queen's). Although the regiment continued to retain the Queen's in its title, it wore Royal Artillery badges and shoulder titles.

THE BUFFS
(ROYAL EAST KENT REGIMENT)

A dragon above a scroll inscribed '*THE BUFFS*'. The badge is in gilding metal.

The regiment derived its name from the buff-coloured coats and breeches worn by the Independent Companies sent by Queen Elizabeth I to the Netherlands to assist the Dutch in their struggle against the Spanish and from which units the Buffs traced their origins.

The dragon in the badge also dated back to the regiment's Elizabethan antecedents, representing a trophy captured from the Spanish during the wars in the Netherlands.

During the Second World War, eleven battalions were raised and all served in an infantry role with the following exceptions:

8th and 11th (formerly 50th) Battalions. These battalions were converted to artillery as the 9th Medium and 89th Light Anti-Aircraft Regiments respectively and wore Royal Artillery cap-badges.

7th Battalion. The 7th Battalion, transferred to the Royal Armoured Corps as the 141st Regiment RAC. However, it continued to wear the dragon cap-badge, albeit in a black beret.

THE KING'S OWN ROYAL REGIMENT (LANCASTER)

The Lion of England on a bar inscribed '*THE KING'S OWN*'. The whole of the badge is in gilding metal.

Badge backing. The badge was backed by a red rectangle. In 1880, as a Royal Regiment, The King's Own was permitted to wear a red insert behind the helmet plate and this, in time, led to the red patch being adopted behind the badge.

Many regiments' badges incorporate a lion, but the King's Own was the only one with the privilege of wearing it on its own. The 'Ancient Badge', the Lion of England, was awarded to the regiment by King William III to commemorate the fact that it was the first unit to join his standard when he landed in Torbay in 1688. From its raising in 1680, the regiment underwent several changes of title before being accorded that of His Majesty's Own Regiment of Foot on the accession of King George I. The title was usually abbreviated to 'The King's Own' as depicted in the wording on the bar below the lion. However, the above title was not adopted until 1881 when the regiment was formally associated with North Lancashire.

In the Second World War the regiment raised ten battalions, but not all remained in an infantry role. Those transferring to other arms included:

4th Battalion. Converted to the 5th (King's Own) Anti-Tank Regiment RA in 1938, the 4th Battalion adopted Royal Artillery badges.

5th Battalion. The 5th Battalion transferred to the Royal Armoured Corps in 1942 as the 107th Regiment RAC (King's Own) but continued to wear its regimental badge. However, instead of a gilding metal badge, a chrome badge was worn and the red backing dispensed with. The regiment was disbanded in 1943.

9th Battalion. This battalion became the 90th Anti-Tank Regiment RA in 1941 and subsequently wore Royal Artillery badges.

10th Battalion. In 1942, the 10th Battalion was converted to armour as the 151st Regiment RAC and wore the Royal Armoured Corps cap-badge. In December 1943, it was re-titled as the 107th (King's Own) Regiment RAC on the disbandment of the former 5th Battalion. Following the change of name, the 10th Battalion reverted to wearing the regimental cap-badge.

THE ROYAL NORTHUMBERLAND FUSILIERS

A grenade, on the ball of which is a circle inscribed '*QUO FATA VOCANT*' (Where the Fates call). Within the circle is a representation of St George killing the dragon. The ball and flame of the grenade are in gilding metal while the circle and the device of St George are in white metal.

Badge backing. In 1943, when the cap GS was introduced, the Royal Northumberland Fusiliers adopted a 2-inch square of gosling green (khaki green), on which was superimposed a red Roman numeral V, as backing for the cap-badge.

The badge of the grenade was common to all fusilier regiments, with each regiment having a distinguishing device on the ball of the grenade. That of the Royal Northumberland Fusiliers dated back to 1675, shortly after the regiment was first raised in the Netherlands, and alluded to its English origins.

The regiment was granted the prefix 'Royal' in 1935 and the above badge was sealed two years later.

In addition to two Regular and four Territorial battalions, the regiment raised a further seven battalions during the Second World War. Not all, however, served in an infantry role nor wore the above badge.

4th Battalion. The 4th Battalion was transferred to the Reconnaissance Corps in April 1941 as its 50th Regiment and adopted a Reconnaissance Corps badge. It served in North Africa and was severely mauled at the Battle of Knightsbridge. Withdrawn from the front-line, it was transferred back to the Royal Northumberland Fusiliers, reclaiming both its battalion number and its regimental badge.

5th Battalion. This Territorial battalion was converted to a searchlight regiment in 1938 and re-titled 53rd Searchlight Regiment RA in August 1940.

In January 1945, the regiment reverted to a 'B' type infantry battalion and was re-titled the 638th Regiment RA (Royal Northumberland Fusiliers). Despite all these changes, the battalion retained its regimental cap-badge.

6th (City) Battalion. Equipped as a tank regiment in 1938, the 6th Battalion was re-titled as the 43rd Battalion, Royal Tank Regiment in 1939, after which it wore the RTR badge. On the expansion of the Territorial Army immediately prior to the Second World War, a duplicate battalion of the 6th had been raised and that, too, became an armoured unit as the 49th Battalion RTR. In 1944 its role changed and its title altered to 49th Armoured Personnel Carrier Regiment RAC. On changing roles, the regiment also changed cap-badges and wore that of the Royal Armoured Corps.

8th Battalion. Like the 4th Battalion, the 8th was converted to a reconnaissance role, becoming the 3rd Regiment, the Reconnaissance Corps in April 1941. It, too, wore Reconnaissance Corps badges although it continued to wear the RNF regimental flash beneath the shoulder titles.

THE ROYAL WARWICKSHIRE REGIMENT

An antelope with a coronet round its neck and a rope attached thereto which is draped towards the front, then over its back, falling to the near side. The antelope stands on ground below which is a wavy scroll inscribed '*ROYAL WARWICKSHIRE*'. The antelope and the coronet are in white metal and the scroll is in gilding metal.

There are two accounts concerning the origin of the regimental badge. One version is that in 1710, at the Battle of Saragossa, the 6th Foot captured a Moorish standard portraying an antelope and this was taken as a regimental emblem. The other relates to the first Colonel of the Regiment, Sir Walter Vane, whose badge was 'an Antelope, ducally gorged and chained'. Whatever the origin, the antelope was confirmed as the badge of the regiment by Royal Warrant in 1743.

The regiment was originally raised in 1674 for service under the Dutch against the French. It was among the forces which accompanied William of Orange when he invaded England in 1688 and was subsequently incorporated into the British Army as the 6th Foot. As the 6th Foot, it had been associated with Warwickshire since 1782 when it was given the secondary title of the 1st Warwickshire Regiment. In 1832, on the direction of King William IV, it was given the prefix 'Royal' and the above title adopted in 1881.

During the Second World War, the Royal Warwickshire Regiment raised six battalions in addition to the existing Regular and Territorial battalions. All served in an infantry role and wore the above cap-badge with the exception of the 13th Battalion which was transferred to the Parachute Regiment in 1942 and became the 8th (Midland Counties) Battalion of that regiment and adopted its cap-badge.

THE ROYAL FUSILIERS
(THE CITY OF LONDON REGIMENT)

A grenade fusee, on the ball of which is the Garter ensigned with an Imperial Crown. Within the Garter is a Tudor Rose. The badge is in gilding metal.

As with all fusilier regiments, the basic badge of the Royal Fusiliers was that of a grenade; the distinguishing device in this case being a Tudor Rose within the Garter.

Unlike the majority of regiments of the line whose connection with the counties in their titles went no further back than the Cardwell Reforms of 1881, the 7th Foot, from which the Royal Fusiliers was directly descended, had always been a London regiment, being formed from the 'Tower Guards' of the Tower of London. The rose and crown motif on the badge reflected the status of the Tower as a royal residence.

During the Second World War the Royal Fusiliers raised a further four battalions, all of which wore the above cap-badge.

In addition, although the 10th (3rd City of London) Battalion became a searchlight regiment in 1938, eventually becoming the 69th Searchlight Regiment RA, it continued to wear its former regimental badge.

THE KING'S REGIMENT (LIVERPOOL)

The White Horse of Hanover in a prancing position, its hind legs on an heraldic torse. Below, a scroll inscribed 'KING'S' in Old English lettering. The horse and torse are in white metal and the scroll is in gilding metal.

Badge backing. From 1944 the 2nd Battalion wore a red square backing behind the badge. The regiment had originally been authorised to wear a red backing to its badge in 1880 in recognition of it being listed among the 'Royal' regiments, which prior to that date had been permitted to wear a red ball tuft on their shakos. Although the practice of wearing the backing was discontinued during the First World War, it was re-introduced into the 2nd Battalion while it was serving in Italy.

The 8th Foot, from which the King's Regiment was descended, had always had royal connections. When raised in 1685 it was designated as Princess Anne of Denmark's Regiment, becoming The King's Regiment of Foot on the accession of King George I. The White Horse of Hanover, which was the main device on the badge, was awarded in 1751, but the above title was not adopted until 1881.

Although in 1936 the King's Regiment consisted of the usual complement of two Regular and four Territorial battalions, by 1939 it was down to only three battalions, two Regular and one Territorial. In the intervening period the other three Territorial battalions had been transferred to other arms and had adopted new badges.

In 1936, the 6th (Rifle) Battalion had been transferred to the Royal Engineers as the 38th (King's) Anti-Aircraft Battalion and ceased to wear the King's badge.

The 7th Battalion was converted to armour in 1939 as 40th (King's) Regiment RAC and although it continued to include its regimental name in its title, it wore the Royal Armoured Corps badge.

Finally, the 10th (Liverpool Scottish) Battalion was transferred to the Corps of the Queen's Own Cameron Highlanders (*qv*) and changed its badge to one which reflected the new relationship.

Even the remaining Territorial battalion, the 5th, went through a metamorphosis. It had originally been a Rifle Volunteer Battalion and had maintained its Rifle traditions through the First World War and up to 1937. It was then persuaded to abandon its blackened badge and conform to the uniform requirements of a normal line regiment.

With the impending outbreak of war the regiment raised three new battalions. These included the 8th (Irish) Battalion (*qv*) and the 9th Battalion, both of which were formed from the nucleus of the 5th.

Following the withdrawal of the BEF from France in 1940, five more battalions were raised, including one, the 14th, on the Isle of Man, but only two of these were destined to remain with the King's Regiment.

11th Battalion. In November 1941, the 11th Battalion was converted to armour as the 152nd Regiment RAC and adopted Royal Armoured Corps badges.

12th Battalion. At the same time as the 11th Battalion was converted to armour, the 12th was transferred to the Royal Artillery as a light anti-aircraft regiment and wore artillery insignia.

15th Battalion. In 1941 the 15th Battalion was transferred to the King's Shropshire Light Infantry as that regiment's 8th Battalion and, on doing so, adopted the badge of the new regiment.

The King's Regiment (Liverpool)
8TH (IRISH) BATALLION

An Irish Harp surmounted by an Imperial Crown and resting on a bed of shamrocks. Below is a scroll inscribed '*8th (IRISH) BN, THE KING'S REGIMENT (LIVERPOOL)*'. The badge is in white metal.

Badge backing. The badge was outlined with a backing of emerald green.

Originally raised in 1860 as the 64th Lancashire Rifle Volunteer Corps from Irishmen living in Liverpool, the 8th (Irish) Battalion first saw active service in the First World War. The battalion was disbanded in 1922, but on the expansion of the Territorial Army in 1939, it was re-formed as a duplicate of the 5th.

While the 8th (Irish) Battalion in the 1914–18 War wore the badge in blackened metal or brass, its Second World War counterpart had the same badge, but in white metal.

The battalion served in the United Kingdom until June 1944 when it participated in the Normandy landings as part of a Beach Group and continued to serve in North West Europe until the end of the war.

THE ROYAL NORFOLK REGIMENT

The figure of Britannia holding a sprig of olive in her right hand and a trident in her left hand. An oval shield bearing the Great Union rests against her left forearm, the whole resting upon a tablet. The badge is in gilding metal.

Badge backing. From 1942, when it joined the 24th Guards Independent Brigade Group, the 1st Battalion wore a black rectangular patch behind the badge.

Like many cap-badges, that of the Royal Norfolk Regiment recalled an outstanding episode in its regimental history. The badge of Britannia was bestowed on the 9th Foot by Queen Anne following the regiment's exemplary gallantry at the Battle of Almanza during the War of the Spanish Succession. It was confirmed as the regiment's 'ancient badge' in 1799.

Following distinguished service in the Great War, the prefix Royal was bestowed on the regiment in 1935.

During the Second World War, the regiment raised nine battalions all of which wore the above badge and, almost uniquely, all served in an infantry role. Of those, no fewer than three Territorial battalions, the 4th, the 5th and the 6th were lost in the Fall of Singapore.

Battalions of the regiment saw service in theatres of war ranging from Europe to the Far East and no fewer than five Victoria Crosses were won.

THE LINCOLNSHIRE REGIMENT

A sphinx resting on a tablet inscribed '*EGYPT*' in Old English lettering, with a scroll beneath inscribed '*LINCOLNSHIRE*'. The sphinx and tablet are in white metal and the scroll is in gilding metal.

The sphinx had been granted to the 10th Foot in 1802 for distinguished service against the French in Egypt and although the regiment had been associated with Lincolnshire since 1792, the above title was not adopted until 1881.

Eight battalions of the regiment served in the Second World War, but only four continued in an infantry role.

Of the others, only one, the 5th Battalion, continued to wear the Lincolnshire cap-badge and this despite several changes of title. In 1938 it became the 46th Searchlight Battalion RE, and was transferred to the Royal Artillery in 1940 as the 46th (Lincolnshire) Searchlight Regiment RA.

The 7th and 8th Battalions also changed to artillery, in 1941 and 1942 respectively, but the 8th only lasted a year in that role, after which it was disbanded and its constituent batteries allocated to other regiments.

The infantry battalions saw active service in three major areas, with the 1st Battalion serving in the Far East and the 6th in the Western Desert and Italy. The 2nd and 4th were involved in Western Europe both before the fall of France and subsequently on the return to Normandy, with the 2nd Battalion taking part in the D-Day landings.

THE DEVONSHIRE REGIMENT

An eight-pointed star, the uppermost point displaced by a crown; on the star a circle inscribed 'THE DEVONSHIRE REGIMENT'. Within the circle, a representation of Exeter Castle above a scroll with the motto 'SEMPER FIDELIS' (Always faithful). The circle and crown are in gilding metal while the star and castle are in white metal.

The Castle of Exeter with the motto 'Semper Fidelis' was a badge worn by the Devonshire Militia and is reputed to commemorate the defence of the city by the County Train Bands during the English Civil War. Unlike many county regiments, the Devonshire Regiment (originally the 11th Foot) had always maintained a connection with the county in which it was first raised in 1685, even though it underwent several changes of name.

The regiment raised eleven battalions during the Second World War and all wore the Devonshire Regiment badge, even though the following battalions were transferred to other arms:

5th Battalion. The original role of this Territorial battalion was that of a machine-gun battalion in the 43rd Division, but in the Autumn of 1941 it was converted to artillery as the 86th Anti-Tank Regiment RA.

7th Battalion. A duplicate battalion of the 5th, the 7th too, became a machine-gun battalion. Similarly, in November 1941, it was converted to artillery as the 87th Anti-Tank Regiment RA.

12th Battalion. In October 1943, the 12th Battalion became part of the air-borne forces in 6th Air Landing Brigade.

THE SUFFOLK REGIMENT

The Castle of Gibraltar, with a scroll above inscribed '*GIBRALTAR*', and a key depending from the centre of the base of the castle and turned to the left, all within a circlet inscribed '*MONTIS INSIGNIA CALPE*' (the badge of the Mount of Calpe – Mount Calpe being the Roman name for Gibraltar). The whole is within an oak-leaf wreath. Above the circlet and between the ends of the wreath is an Imperial Crown; below the circlet and resting on the base of the wreath, a scroll inscribed '*THE SUFFOLK REGIMENT*'. The badge is in white metal except for the scroll which is in gilding metal.

Badge backing. A red insert was worn behind the voided centre of the badge. This was introduced in the 1920s but appears to have been unofficial even though all battalions adopted the practice.

The regiment was raised in 1685, becoming the 12th Foot in 1751. It took a significant part in the defence of Gibraltar during the Great Siege (1779–83) and for its gallantry there was awarded the battle-honour 'Gibraltar' which figured so prominently in the design of the cap-badge. The regiment's connections with Suffolk extended back to 1782, but the current title was not bestowed until 1881 when the above badge was adopted.

During the Second World War the regiment raised eleven battalions, all of which wore the above cap-badge. Even the 7th Battalion, which transferred to the Royal Armoured Corps as 142nd Regiment RAC, continued to wear the Suffolk cap-badge, even though other RAC insignia were worn.

The Suffolks served in all major theatres of war, even though losing two Territorial battalions in the Fall of Singapore.

The Suffolk Regiment
THE CAMBRIDGESHIRE REGIMENT

The Castle of Cambridge, on the central tower of which is a shield bearing the Arms of Ely; below, a scroll inscribed '*THE CAMBRIDGESHIRE REGIMENT*'. The castle and the coat of arms are in white metal and the scroll is in gilding metal.

Prior to the Cardwell Reforms there had been a Regular regiment associated with Cambridgeshire, the 30th Foot, but in 1881 it became the 1st Battalion of the newly-formed East Lancashire Regiment. However, there had been no replacement of a Regular regiment in the county and the 'new' Cambridgeshire Regiment was formed from the 3rd Battalion of the Suffolk Regiment on the establishment of the Territorial Force in 1908. The Cambridgeshire Regiment thus became one of only four 'regiments' in the Territorial Army, although it still retained its links with its parent regiment, the Suffolks.

The current badge was adopted on the regiment's formation in 1908.

During the Second World War, the Cambridgeshire Regiment raised two battalions, both of which served in the ill-fated 18th Division which arrived in Singapore almost simultaneously with the Japanese in 1942.

An official escape party from the 2nd Battalion left Singapore after the surrender in the hope of reaching Allied lines in India and thus forming the nucleus of a third battalion. The party disappeared and no further battalions of the regiment were formed.

THE SOMERSET LIGHT INFANTRY (PRINCE ALBERT'S)

A strung bugle-horn, mouth-piece to the right, with the initials 'PA' in ornamental lettering between the strings. Above the badge is a mural crown superscribed 'JELLALABAD' on a scroll. The badge is in white metal.

Badge backing. From 1943, on the introduction of the cap GS, the badge was backed by a square of Light Infantry green.

Raised in 1685, the regiment was numbered 13th Foot in 1751, to which the secondary title of 1st Somersetshire was added in 1782. In 1822 the regiment was converted to Light Infantry and the bugle, a device common to all Light Infantry regiments, was incorporated into the badge.

In 1842 the regiment was awarded a mural crown superscribed 'Jellalabad' to commemorate its gallantry during the siege of that town in the First Afghan War. At the same time it was granted a royal tide, becoming Prince Albert's Regiment of Light Infantry and this latter honour is reflected in the initials 'PA' in the bugle strings.

Although the above badge was authorised in 1881, the title was not adopted until 1920.

The Second World War saw the regiment raise ten battalions, all of which originally wore the same cap-badge. However, the 7th Battalion was transferred to the Parachute Regiment on its formation in 1942 and adopted the latter badge.

THE WEST YORKSHIRE REGIMENT
(THE PRINCE OF WALES'S OWN)

The White Horse of Hanover in a galloping attitude on ground. Below the ground a scroll inscribed 'WEST YORKSHIRE'. The White Horse and ground are in white metal and the scroll is in gilding metal.

The 14th Foot was awarded the badge of the White Horse of Hanover for service to the House of Hanover, service which included action during the Battle of Culloden. Its secondary title, 'the Prince of Wales's Own', was conferred on the regiment in 1876 and it was given the above title in 1881.

Eleven battalions served in the Second World War and all wore the above badge with the following exceptions:

2/5th Battalion. Raised in 1939 from the original 5th Battalion, the 2/5th was transferred to the Royal Armoured Corps in 1942 as the 113rd Regiment RAC and wore the badge of its new corps.

6th Battalion. The 6th Battalion was transferred to the Royal Engineers in 1936 and then, in 1940, transferred to the Royal Artillery, becoming 49th Searchlight Regiment RA and wearing artillery badges.

7th (Leeds Rifles) Battalion. On the doubling of the Territorial Army in 1939, the Leeds Rifles again divided in to two battalions, the 7th and 8th. The 7th Battalion was converted to armour and in 1940 it became 45th Royal Tank Regiment and adopted RTR badges.

8th (Leeds Rifles) Battalion. The 8th Battalion had never worn the above badge and a description of this battalion's badge appears in Section III.

THE EAST YORKSHIRE REGIMENT
(THE DUKE OF YORK'S OWN)

An eight-pointed star with the White Rose of York in the centre, the rose encircled by a laurel wreath. Below the star is a scroll inscribed '*EAST YORKSHIRE*'. The rose is in white metal and the remainder of the badge is in gilding metal.

The 15th Foot was raised in 1685 but its association with Yorkshire was first recognised in 1792 when it became the East Riding Regiment. Although the connection with the East Riding was maintained, the title was amended in 1881 when the current name and badge were adopted. The secondary title of 'The Duke of York's Own' was conferred on the regiment to mark the Silver Jubilee of King George V in 1935.

The device of the White Rose of York was common to the majority of Yorkshire regiments and was depicted on the badges of both Regular and Militia battalions of the regiment from the middle of the nineteenth century.

Seven battalions of the East Yorkshire Regiment served in the Second World War and all wore the above cap-badge.

The 8th Battalion, however, did not serve as infantry, being converted to artillery in January 1942 as the 115th Light Anti-Aircraft Regiment RA.

THE BEDFORDSHIRIE AND HERTFORDSHIRE REGIMENT

The Cross of the Order of the Bath superimposed upon the Star of the Order of the Garter. In the centre is the Garter and motto, within which is a hart crossing a ford; below all is a scroll inscribed '*BEDFORDSHIRE AND HERTFORDSHIRE*'. The badge is in white metal.

The 16th Foot was originally raised in 1688, but the regiment's association with Bedfordshire dates from 1809. In 1881 it became the Bedfordshire Regiment when the above badge was adopted, although the scroll was amended in 1919.

The badge draws on three main sources for its composition. The first, the Cross of the Order of the Bath was conferred on the Earl of Deloraine in 1725 when he was colonel of the regiment and the badge is traditionally associated with this honour. There seems to be no specific reason why the second of the two devices, the Star and motto of the Garter, was adopted, for it did not appear on any of the Bedfordshire badges prior to the Cardwell Reforms. The central device, a hart crossing a ford, was incorporated in 1881 when the Hertfordshire Militia became the 4th Battalion of the Bedfordshire Regiment.

The association between the two counties, recognised in both Militia and Territorial Force battalions, was further reinforced during the Great War when many Hertfordshire men enlisted in the Bedfordshire Regiment. In recognition of this, 'Hertfordshire' was incorporated into the regimental title under AO 269 of 1919 and the amended scroll introduced.

During the Second World War, the regiment raised five battalions. The 1st, 2nd and 5th wore the above badge, while the other two battalions wore the badge of the Hertfordshire Regiment (*qv*).

The Bedfordshire and Hertfordshire Regiment
THE HERTFORDSHIRE REGIMENT

A hart lodged in water within a circlet inscribed *THE HERTFORDSHIRE REGIMENT*, the whole surmounted by an Imperial Crown. The badge is in gilding metal.

The Hertfordshire Regiment traced its origins back to the various Corps of Rifle Volunteers which were raised in the county in 1859–60 and which, in 1880, were formed into the 1st and 2nd Hertfordshire Rifle Volunteer Corps. Both these units wore a badge in which the main device was a hart in water, the Arms of the Borough of Hertford.

In 1887 the two Rifle Volunteer Corps were absorbed into the Bedfordshire Regiment as the 1st and 2nd Hertfordshire Volunteer battalions and wore badges very similar to that of their Regular counterparts. However, in 1908, on the formation of the Territorial Force, the two battalions were united into the Hertfordshire Regiment, one of only four Territorial 'regiments' to be so nominated. The above badge, based on those worn by the nineteenth century Rifle Volunteers, was then adopted.

Despite the change in the title of the Bedfordshire Regiment in 1919, the Hertfordshire Regiment continued to maintain a separate identity as a Territorial component within the corps of the parent regiment.

The Hertfordshire Regiment raised two battalions during the Second World War and both wore the above badge.

THE LEICESTERSHIRE REGIMENT

The Royal Tiger on ground superscribed '*HINDOOSTAN*' and a scroll below inscribed '*LEICESTERSHIRE*'. The Tiger and ground are in gilding metal and the scrolls are in white metal.

The 17th Foot, which became the Leicestershire Regiment in 1881, was granted the Royal Tiger and the inscription 'Hindoostan' for services in India between 1804 and 1823.

Prior to 1936 the regiment had two Regular and two Territorial battalions. In December 1936, however, the 4th Battalion was converted to a searchlight unit. The remaining Territorial battalion was doubled up in 1938 to form the 1/5th and 2/5th and a further three battalions were formed on the outbreak of war.

With the exception of the 4th Battalion, all other battalions served in an infantry role and wore the above badge.

The 4th Battalion was transferred to the Royal Engineers in 1936 as the 44th (The Leicestershire Regiment) Anti-Aircraft Battalion RE. The battalion was transferred to the Royal Artillery in 1940 and although any reference to its regimental origin disappeared from its title, the Leicestershire Regiment badge continued to be worn throughout the war.

THE GREEN HOWARDS
(ALEXANDRA, PRINCESS OF WALES'S OWN
YORKSHIRE REGIMENT)

The letter *A*, cypher of the late Queen Alexandra, with '*ALEXANDRA*' inscribed on the crossbar of the cypher. Combined with the cypher is the Dannebrog, the national symbol of Denmark, with '*1875*' inscribed on the cross. Below the cypher is a scroll inscribed '*THE PRINCESS OF WALES'S OWN YORKSHIRE REGIMENT*', the word Yorkshire forming a straight base for the cypher, and a rose in the centre of the scroll. The badge is ensigned with an Imperial Crown. The badge is in white metal.

Badge backing. When worn in the cap OS, the badge was backed by a grass green patch.

The Green Howards was raised in 1689, and had a long connection with the North Riding of Yorkshire; reference to the area survived in the title until 1881, when the above title was adopted. The only device remaining in the badge after that date which associated the regiment with Yorkshire was the White Rose of York in the centre of the scroll.

The main device relates to the late Queen Alexandra, consort of King Edward VII. It consists of her cypher, the letter 'A' interwoven with the Dannebrog, or Danish Cross, which symbolised her Danish ancestry. The date, 1875, refers to the year in which the regiment was granted its secondary title.

The regiment raised eleven battalions during the Second World War and all wore the above cap-badge except those indicated below:

9th Battalion. The 9th Battalion was transferred to the Royal Artillery in 1941 as the 108th Light Anti-Aircraft Regiment and subsequently wore the RA cap-badge.

10th Battalion. Transferred to the Parachute Regiment in June 1943 as the 12th (Yorkshire) Battalion, the Parachute Regiment, the 10th Battalion adopted the cap-badge of that regiment.

12th Battalion. Initially the 12th Battalion was transferred to the Royal Armoured Corps as the 161st Regiment RAC and wore armoured corps insignia. In October 1943, however, it returned to an infantry role as the 161st (Green Howards) Regiment, the Reconnaissance Corps, and wore the latter's badge.

THE LANCASHIRE FUSILIERS

A grenade, on the ball of which is a sphinx resting on a tablet inscribed 'EGYPT' and surrounded by a laurel wreath. Below the grenade is a scroll inscribed 'THE LANCASHIRE FUSILIERS'. The grenade is in gilding metal and the scroll is in white metal.

The grenade of the Lancashire Fusiliers' badge displayed the distinguishing device of the sphinx and a laurel wreath, both of which represented battle-honours awarded to the regiment. The badge of the sphinx was granted to the 20th Foot in 1802 for service against the French in Egypt. The wreath pre-dated this and was awarded to the regiment to commemorate its action at the Battle of Minden in 1759.

Originally raised in 1688, the regiment had had an association with Devonshire and did not receive the above title until the Cardwell Reforms of 1881.

The Lancashire Fusiliers raised twelve battalions during the Second World War and with the exception of the 7th, all wore the above cap-badge, even when not serving in an infantry role.

Three battalions, the 1/5th, 1/6th and the 9th were transferred to the Royal Armoured Corps in 1941 and although the black beret of the RAC was worn, all three continued to wear the Lancashire Fusiliers' cap-badge.

The 7th Battalion was transferred to the Royal Artillery and subsequently wore the RA cap-badge.

THE ROYAL SCOTS FUSILIERS

A grenade on which there are the Royal Arms. The badge is in gilding metal.

Badge backing. The badge was backed by a square of 42nd, or Government, tartan, although the pipers of the regiment wore the (red) Erskine tartan.

The badge of the Royal Scots Fusiliers, like that of all fusilier regiments, was that of a grenade. The differences occurred in both the size and the device on the ball of the grenade. That of the Royal Scots Fusiliers was approximately four times larger than that of any other fusilier regiment and the size, together with the Royal Arms on the grenade, reflected the regiment's ranking as the senior regiment of fusiliers.

The regiment was raised in 1678 as the 21st Foot and was designated as fusiliers by 1691 with the title of the Royal North British Fusiliers. The above title was not adopted until 1881 and the current badge was not introduced until the accession of King Edward VII in 1901, when the Royal Crest replaced Queen Victoria's crown above the Royal Arms.

Three battalions of the regiment served in the Second World War and all wore the above badge.

THE CHESHIRE REGIMENT

On an eight-pointed star, a circlet inscribed '*THE CHESHIRE REGIMENT*'. Within the circlet is an acorn in the vertical position between oak-leaves, while on the inside of the outer rim is a rope motif. The centre of the badge is in gilding metal and the star is in white metal.

The above badge dated only from 1922, but the acorn and oak-leaves had always featured prominently on the cap-badge and colours of the Cheshire Regiment. They are held to commemorate an incident at Dettingen during the War of the Austrian Succession, when a detachment of the 22nd Foot, which later became the Cheshire Regiment, was able to prevent the capture of King George II by the French. However, an alternative origin of the oak-leaves may be ascribed to the fact that the coat of arms of the regiment's first commanding officer, the Duke of Norfolk, contained a sprig of acorn.

Before the Second World War the Cheshire Regiment consisted of two Regular and two Territorial battalions. In 1939 the Territorial battalions were doubled, the 4th/5th dividing into two battalions, as they had been prior to 1920, while the 6th Battalion, which had been converted to artillery between the wars, returned to the regiment as an infantry battalion.

All six battalions wore the above badge.

THE ROYAL WELCH FUSILIERS

A grenade, on the ball of which is a circle inscribed '*ROYAL WELCH FUSILIERS*'. Within the circle are the Prince of Wales's plumes with coronet and motto. The grenade and coronet are in gilding metal and the remainder of the badge is in white metal.

The grenade badge of the Royal Welch Fusiliers was distinguished from those other fusilier regiments by the Prince of Wales's plumes and coronet on the ball. In addition, it had two tiers of flames emanating from the grenade instead of the usual one.

The regiment was raised in 1689, becoming the 23rd Foot in 1751. However, both its connection with Wales and its status as a fusilier regiment had been confirmed as early as 1713 when it became the Royal Regiment of Welch Fusiliers. Subsequently, the word 'Welch' was replaced in the nineteenth century by the word 'Welsh' in official usage although the regiment preferred the original spelling and attempted to have it re-accepted. This was finally achieved in 1920 when the above title and cap-badge were adopted.

During the Second World War, the regiment raised fifteen battalions, all of which, with the following exceptions, wore the above badge:

5th Battalion. The 5th Battalion was converted to artillery in 1940 as the 60th Anti-Tank Regiment RA and wore Royal Artillery badges.

19th (Merionethshire and Montgomeryshire) Battalion. Raised in 1939 as a duplicate of the 7th Battalion, the 10th became the 6th (Royal Welch) Battalion, the Parachute Regiment in July 1942 and adopted the cap-badge of that regiment.

THE SOUTH WALES BORDERERS

Within an unbroken wreath of immortelles, a sphinx resting on a tablet inscribed '*EGYPT*'. On the lower portion of the wreath are the letters '*SWB*'. The wreath is in gilding metal and the remainder of the badge is in white metal.

The grant of the sphinx was made to the 24th Foot for its service against the French in Egypt during the Napoleonic Wars. The wreath of immortelles around the sphinx commemorated the award of a wreath of such flowers to the 1st Battalion of the regiment by Queen Victoria in 1880 in recognition of its stand against the Zulus at Isandhlwana.

During the Second World War, the regiment raised five battalions, excluding the battalions of the Monmouthshire Regiment (*qv*). The above badge was worn by the 1st, 2nd and 5th Battalions, the other two wearing the badges of the arms to which they were transferred.

6th Battalion. Converted to armour as the 158th Regiment RAC in 1942, the 6th Battalion wore Royal Armoured Corps badges until it reverted to its original role and title in 1943.

7th Battalion. The 7th Battalion converted to artillery in October 1941 after which it wore Royal Artillery badges.

The South Wales Borderers
2ND and 3RD BATTALIONS, THE
MONMOUTHSHIRE REGIMENT

A Welsh Dragon on ground. The badge is in gilding metal.

The Monmouthshire Regiment originated as a Volunteer Battalion of the South Wales Borderers, but in 1908 became one of the four 'regiments' of infantry in the Territorial Force. In 1929 an Army Order laid down that the Monmouthshire Regiment again become part of the corps of the South Wales Borderers.

The badge of the Welsh Dragon was introduced in 1908 on the establishment of the regiment, but the 1st Battalion changed its badge in 1925 to incorporate the battle-honours awarded in the Great War. However, the 2nd and 3rd Battalions continued to wear the above badge.

Between the two world wars the Monmouthshire Regiment maintained three infantry battalions, but in 1938 the 1st Battalion was transferred to the Royal Engineers as a searchlight unit.

On the expansion of the Territorial Army in 1939 two further battalions of the regiment were raised, but shortly after their formation both these new battalions were transferred to the South Wales Borderers and wore the latter's badge.

The 2nd and 3rd Battalions continued to wear the Dragon badge and, after serving in the United Kingdom until 1944, both saw active service in the North West Europe Campaign.

THE KING'S OWN SCOTTISH BORDERERS

Within a circle inscribed '*KING'S OWN SCOTTISH BORDERERS*', the Castle of Edinburgh with flags flying to the left from the top of each tower; above the circle, a scroll inscribed with the motto '*IN VERITATE RELIGIONIS CONFIDO*' (In true religion is my trust) and below the circle, a second scroll with the motto '*NISI DOMINUS FRUSTRA*' (Unless the Lord is with me, all is in vain). Outside the circle is a wreath of thistles with the Royal Crest above the first motto; the Cross of St Andrew overall and intertwined with the circle and the scrolls. The badge is in white metal.

Badge backing. The badge was backed by a 3-inch square of Leslie tartan except for that of the pipers who wore a Royal Stuart tartan.

The regiment traced its origins back to the 25th Foot (The King's Own Borderers) which was raised in Edinburgh in 1689, hence the representation of Edinburgh Castle and the two mottoes of that city in its badge. The above title and badge were, however, not adopted until 1887. Under the Cardwell Reforms of 1881 it had been the intention to make the Depot and Headquarters of the 25th at York and for the regiment to become a Militia battalion of the East Yorkshire Regiment. The 25th protested strongly that it was a Scottish regiment and eventually it was agreed that it could be so regarded, but its Depot was to be in Berwick on Tweed which was, and is, an English town.

In 1887 it was realised by the War Office that the King's Own Borderers did not have a Militia battalion and the 3rd Battalion the Royal Scots Fusiliers was transferred to become the Militia battalion of the regiment. Traditionally, the 3rd (Militia) Battalion of the Royal Scots Fusiliers had been known as the Scottish Borderers Militia and on the transfer, the opportunity was taken to introduce the word 'Scottish' into the title of the new parent regiment.

The above badge, reflecting the change of name was introduced at the same time.

Concurrently with these changes, the King's Own Scottish Borderers, in common with other Lowland regiments, was obliged to incorporate tartan, which until then had been the preserve of the Highland regiments, into its uniform. Initially the Government tartan was worn, but in 1898 authorisation was given to wear the Leslie tartan in commemoration of the Earl of Leven who had originally raised the regiment. Thus when the practice of wearing the tartan patch behind the badge was introduced, it was appropriate that the Leslie tartan was used.

During the Second World War six battalions were raised in addition to the two Regular battalions. Apart from two, which were designated home defence battalions, all the remainder saw active service as infantry – none being transferred to other arms.

No variations to the above badge were worn.

THE CAMERONIANS (THE SCOTTISH RIFLES)

A mullet (a five-pointed star) above a stringed bugle; arising from each end of the bugle and enclosing the mullet, a spray of thistles. The badge is in white metal.

Badge backing. The badge was backed by a 3-inch square patch of Douglas tartan. However, a black hackle was apparently worn in lieu of the cap-badge by the 1st Battalion while serving in the Far East.

The 1st Battalion of the Cameronians (formerly the 26th Foot) was raised in 1688 and was named after the Covenanter leader, Richard Cameron, although the mullet in the badge and its tartan backing are taken from the Douglas family, as it was from the tenants of the Douglas estates that the first members of the regiment were recruited. In 1881, the 26th Foot was merged with the Perthshire Volunteers Light Infantry, the 90th Foot, which is represented in the badge by the strung bugle, common to all Light Infantry regiments.

During the Second World War, six battalions of the regiment saw active service while a further four battalions were raised for home defence and training duties.

With the exception of the 5th/8th Battalion, all served in an infantry role.

The 5th/8th Battalion became a searchlight unit in 1938, transferring to the Royal Artillery in 1940 as the 56th Searchlight Regiment RA. However, although the regiment adopted artillery shoulder titles, it continued to wear the badge of the Cameronians.

THE ROYAL INNISKILLING FUSILIERS

A grenade, on the ball of which is depicted the Castle of Enniskillen with St George's flag flying to the right from the central tower. Below the castle is a scroll inscribed *'INNISKILLING'*. The grenade is in gilding metal and the castle and scroll are in white metal.

Badge backing. The badge was backed by a red triangle which was adopted after the Great War to commemorate the distinguished service of the 1st Battalion at Gallipoli with the 29th Division, whose divisional sign was a red triangle. In addition, the regiment wore a grey hackle behind the badge in recognition of its forbears' participation in the Defence of Enniskilling in 1689.

The regiment was raised by King William III from the defenders of Enniskillen after the raising of the siege of the town in 1689, hence the representation of the castle of Enniskillen and the scroll on the ball of the grenade.

The regiment raised three additional battalions during the Second World War and all wore the above badge, none being transferred to other arms.

The 2nd and 6th Battalions of the regiment were both engaged on the Italian front and after severe losses on the Garrigliano and at Monte Cassino, they were withdrawn to Egypt. Here they were amalgamated and the re-formed 2nd Battalion returned to Italy for the later stages of the campaign and the advance into Austria.

THE GLOUCESTERSHIRE REGIMENT

The sphinx resting upon a tablet inscribed '*EGYPT*' within two sprigs of laurel. Below the laurel is a scroll inscribed '*GLOUCESTERSHIRE*'. The badge is in white metal.

Badge backing. The back badge consists of a sphinx upon a tablet inscribed '*EGYPT*' all within a laurel wreath. The badge is in gilding metal.

The Gloucestershire Regiment was formed in 1881 from two existing regiments with Gloucestershire connections: the 28th Foot (The North Gloucestershire Regiment) and the 61st (The South Gloucestershire Regiment). It is from the former that the regiment derived its unique distinction of wearing a second miniature badge at the back of the head-dress. The honour was bestowed on the 28th Foot for its actions against the French in Egypt in 1801, service which is also alluded to in the main device of the badge: the sphinx on a tablet inscribed 'Egypt'.

During the Second World War, the Gloucestershire Regiment raised eleven battalions and, except where indicated below, all wore the above badge (and back badge).

4th (City of Bristol) Battalion. Transferred to the Royal Engineers as a searchlight battalion in November 1938, the 4th Battalion subsequently became the 66th Searchlight Regiment RA and wore Royal Artillery badges.

6th Battalion. The 6th Battalion was converted to armour in early 1938 as the 44th Regiment, Royal Tank Corps and wore RTC badges. On the creation of the Royal Tank Regiment in 1939, the battalion changed to the new insignia.

10th Battalion. During the period July 1942 to April 1943, the battalion served in the Royal Armoured Corps as 150th Regiment RAC and wore the badge of that corps. It reverted to an infantry role in April 1943 and assumed its original designation and Gloucestershire badges.

11th Battalion. In February 1942, the 11th Battalion was converted to artillery as the 118th Light Anti-Aircraft Regiment RA and adopted Royal Artillery badges.

The back badge of the Gloucestershire Regiment

THE WORCESTERSHIRE REGIMENT

An elongated eight-pointed star. On this, the Garter proper and within this the Lion of England standing upon a tablet inscribed 'FIRM'. The Garter is in gilding metal and the remainder of the badge is in white metal.

Badge backing. An emerald green rectangle was worn behind the badge on the cap GS.

The badge of the Worcestershire Regiment incorporated elements from the badges of both the 29th and 36th Foot which amalgamated to form the regiment in 1881.

The shape of the badge was probably derived from 29th Foot's association with the Coldstream Guards – an association which originated from the raising of the regiment in 1694 by Colonel Farrington of the Coldstream Guards, which regiment also supplied a number of later commanding officers. From the 29th Foot also came the Lion of England.

The 36th Foot, which became the 2nd Battalion, contributed the motto '0Firm'. The origin of this motto and how the 36th Foot became entitled to it are unknown, but it was used as the Regimental Seal as early as 1773.

At the end of the Garter buckle there is, instead of the usual ornamentation, a representation of three pears. These were drawn from the arms of the City of Worcester and alluded to what was once the major industry in the county – the perry orchards.

In the Second World War, the regiment raised six battalions as well as its two Regular battalions. Only one, the 12th, was transferred to another arm, becoming the 179th Field Regiment RA in February 1942, after which it wore Royal Artillery badges.

THE EAST LANCASHIRE REGIMENT

A sphinx resting upon a tablet inscribed '*EGYPT*'. Below the tablet is a rose and the whole is within a laurel wreath which is ensigned with an Imperial Crown. Resting upon the lower portion of the wreath is a scroll inscribed '*EAST LANCASHIRE*'. The badge is in white metal, except for the rose which is in gilding metal.

Prior to 1881 neither of the two regiments which were combined to form the East Lancashire Regiment had had any connection with Lancashire. The 30th Foot, which became the 1st Battalion, had originally been associated with Cambridgeshire, while the 59th Foot, the new second regiment's 2nd Battalion, had been a Nottinghamshire Regiment.

The sphinx in the badge was drawn from that of the 30th Foot which had been awarded the honour for service in Egypt against the French in the Napoleonic Wars. The rose represents the Red Rose of Lancaster incorporated into the badge to reinforce the regiment's association with its county of adoption.

In addition to its two Regular and two Territorial battalions, the regiment raised three new battalions during the Second World War. However, of the three, two were very shortly transferred to other arms.

7th Battalion. The 7th Battalion became a Light Anti-Aircraft Regiment in 1941 and on doing so adopted the badges of the Royal Artillery.

8th Battalion. Converted to armour in 1942, the 8th Battalion initially became the 144th Regiment, Royal Armoured Corps. Later, it was re-designated the 44th Royal Tank Regiment. Although it retained the East Lancashire Regiment badge for a time, it subsequently wore the badge of the Royal Tank Regiment.

THE EAST SURREY REGIMENT

An eight-pointed star, the top point being displaced by an Imperial Crown which rests upon a shield being the Arms of Guildford (i.e. the Castle of Guildford with a lion couchant in front of the castle and a woolpack at either side). Below is a scroll inscribed 'EAST SURREY'. The star and castle are in white metal and the remainder of the badge is in gilding metal.

Neither of the two regiments which formed the East Surrey Regiment in 1881 had had any prior connection with their county of adoption: the 1st Battalion originated in Huntingdonshire as the 31st Foot, while the 2nd Battalion (the former 70th Foot) had Scottish antecedents. Because of this lack of association, the new regiment took the coat of arms of the county town as the main device in its badge in order to establish a better relationship with the county of its adoption.

Nine battalions of the regiment served in the Second World War and all wore the above badge.

Two other battalions, the former 5th and 7th, were transferred out of the regiment prior to the outbreak of war, the 5th Battalion becoming an artillery regiment and the 7th eventually becoming the 42nd Battalion, the Royal Tank Regiment. Each adopted the badge of its new arm.

THE DUKE OF CORNWALL'S LIGHT INFANTRY

The main device is strung bugle, common to all Light Infantry regiments. Above the bugle is a scroll resting on each end of the bugle. The scroll is inscribed 'CORNWALL' and is surmounted by a representation of the ducal coronet of the Duke of Cornwall, the hereditary title of the Prince of Wales, when in the Duchy of Cornwall. The badge is in white metal.

Badge backing. The 2nd Battalion wore a red insert behind the voided centre of the badge. This commemorates a successful night attack on the colonist forces by a number of light companies of the 46th Foot (later to become the 2nd Battalion, the Duke of Cornwall's Light Infantry) at Paoli on 20 September 1777. Initially the backing took the form of a tuft of red feathers, worn to advise the colonial forces that it was the 46th Foot that had carried out the attack and not any other regiment.

Although the 32nd Foot had been associated with Cornwall since 1782, it did not become a Light Infantry Corps until after the Indian Mutiny when the bugle was adopted. In 1881 the 32nd Foot became the 1st Battalion, the Duke of Cornwall's Light Infantry but because the regiment had no association with the Battle of Paoli Bridge it did not wear the red insert, which remained the privilege of the 2nd Battalion. However, from 1943 the 1st Battalion, in common with the majority of other light infantry regiments, adopted a green patch behind the badge.

During the Second World War, the regiment raised seven battalions, all of which remained in an infantry role and wore the above badge.

THE DUKE OF WELLINGTON'S REGIMENT (WEST RIDING)

The crest, ducal coronet and motto of the Duke of Wellington above a scroll inscribed '*THE WEST RIDING*'. The crest and motto are in white metal and the scroll is in gilding metal.

Badge backing. A red cloth backing, consisting of a triangle with rounded corners, was worn behind the badge. Although the shape was only introduced in 1943 with the introduction of the cap GS, a red patch had been worn for many years previously to commemorate the exploits of the regiment's Light Company at the Battle of Brandywine during the American War of independence.

The Duke of Wellington's Regiment was unique in that it was the only regiment in the British Army which was named after a commoner. The Duke of Wellington had had a long association with both the 33rd and 76th Regiments of Foot and this association was recalled in the badge which they adopted on their amalgamation in 1881. The badge incorporates the Duke's crest and motto: '*Virtutis Fortuna Comes*' (Fortune favours the brave) and although the above title was not adopted until 1920, the association of the regiment with the West Riding extended back to 1782 when the 33rd Foot adopted the secondary title of 1st Yorkshire, West Riding Regiment.

The Duke of Wellington's Regiment raised fourteen battalions during the Second World War and of these no fewer than seven were transferred to other arms, although two subsequently returned to the regiment.

1/4th Battalion was converted to artillery as the 58th (Duke of Wellington's Regiment) Anti-Tank Regiment in 1939 and wore Royal Artillery badges.

2/4th Battalion. Like the 1/4th, the 2/4th Battalion was transferred to the Royal Artillery in 1939 as the 68th (Duke of Wellington's Regiment) Anti-Tank Regiment and wore artillery badges.

5th Battalion. The third Territorial battalion of the Duke of Wellington's Regiment to convert to artillery, the 5th Battalion became the 43rd Searchlight Regiment RA and, like the other two battalions, wore Royal Artillery badges.

2/6th Battalion. After seeing action with the BEF in 1940 as an infantry battalion, the 2/6th was converted to armour in 1942 as the 114th Regiment RAC and wore Royal Armoured Corps badges. However, in 1944 it was re-formed as infantry and became the 11th Battalion of its parent regiment – and regained its regimental badge.

2/7th Battalion. The pattern of the 2/7th Battalion followed closely that of the 2/6th. After serving in France in 1940, it was transferred to the Royal Armoured Corps as the 115th Regiment RAC in 1942. In 1944 it returned to the Duke of Wellington's Regiment as its 12th Battalion and re-adopted the regimental badge.

8th and 9th Battalions. The two battalions were also transferred to the Royal Armoured Corps as the 145th and 146th Regiments RAC. Unlike the 2/6th and 2/7th Battalions, they did not revert to an infantry role and continued to wear RAC insignia throughout the war.

THE BORDER REGIMENT

The Star of the Order of the Garter, but with an Imperial Crown displacing the uppermost point. On the star, a cross on the four arms of which are displayed the battle-honours of the regiment. In the centre of the cross, a circle inscribed '*ARROYO DOS MOLINOS 1811*' and within the circle, a dragon superscribed '*CHINA*'. Interposed between the star and the cross is a laurel wreath and on the three lowest points of the star, a scroll inscribed '*THE BORDER REGIMENT*'. The badge is in white metal.

Badge backing. A red insert was worn behind the voided centre of the badge to represent the plume granted the 34th Foot (later the 1st Battalion of the Border Regiment) for its outstanding conduct at the Battle of Arroyo dos Molinos during the Peninsular Wars.

The Border Regiment was formed in 1881 by an amalgamation of the 34th Foot (Cumberland Regiment) and the 55th Foot (Westmorland Regiment) and the lowest arm of the badge records the first battle-honour of the amalgamated regiment: the Relief of Ladysmith. The centre of the badge records the main battle-honour of each of the constituent regiments. As already indicated, the battle-honour of Arroyo dos Molinos was awarded to the 34th Foot, while the Dragon was awarded to the 55th Foot for service in the China War of 1840–42.

During the Second World War the regiment raised ten battalions, all but one continuing to serve in an infantry role.

The 5th Battalion was converted to armour in September 1941, becoming 110th Regiment RAC (The Border Regiment). Even so, the battalion retained its Border Regiment cap-badge until it was disbanded in 1943.

THE ROYAL SUSSEX REGIMENT

The Star of the Order of the Garter over the Roussillon plume with a scroll below inscribed '*THE ROYAL SUSSEX REGIMENT*'. The badge is in white metal and the scroll is in gilding metal.

The Royal Sussex Regiment was originally raised in Belfast in 1701 as the 35th Foot, although the regiment's association with that city was not maintained. In 1805, the regiment was finally allocated to Sussex and was subsequently granted the prefix 'Royal' in 1832 before being amalgamated with the 107th Foot (Bengal Infantry) in 1881.

It was from the action of the 35th Foot that the badge of the Royal Sussex draws the distinctive Roussillon plume. In the battle for Quebec in 1759, the regiment defeated the French Roussillon Regiment and personnel of the 35th, removed the plumes from the hats of their enemies and stuck them in their own. However, the plume was not incorporated into the badge until 1901.

Unlike the majority of county regiments which drew the main device of their badges from those of the Regiments of Foot from which they were formed in 1881, that of the badge of the Royal Sussex Regiment, the Star of the Order of the Garter, was adopted because the Duke of Richmond had had the order conferred upon him while commanding the Sussex Militia.

Ten battalions of the Royal Sussex Regiment served in the Second World War and with the exceptions noted below, all wore the above badge.

5th (Cinque Ports) Battalion. (*qv*)

7th Battalion. On becoming the 109th Light Anti-Aircraft Regiment RA in 1940, the 7th Battalion adopted Royal Artillery cap-badges.

The Royal Sussex Regiment
5TH (CINQUE PORTS) BATTALION

A Maltese Cross, similar to that in the Order of the Bath, but without the lions in the angles, in front of the Roussillon plume. In the centre of the cross, a circle bearing the Arms of the Cinque Ports. Below the cross is a scroll inscribed 'CINQUE PORTS'. The badge is in gilding metal.

The Cinque Ports Battalion of the Royal Sussex Regiment traced its origins back to the Volunteers which had been raised in the mid-nineteenth century. Its badge differed from the Regular cap-badge in that, although it retained the Roussillon plume, it had a Maltese Cross, similar to the Order of the Bath, instead of the Star of the Order of the Garter. In the centre of the cross was a shield bearing the Arms of the Cinque Ports, from which towns the majority of the personnel of the battalion were recruited.

The badge was officially authorised in 1909 after the formation of the Territorial Force.

Although the 7th (Cinque Ports) battalion was raised as a duplicate of the 5th in 1939, it did not wear the above badge, but wore the standard regimental badge until its conversion to artillery in 1940.

THE HAMPSHIRE REGIMENT

The Hampshire Rose with, above, the Royal Tiger standing on a torse, the whole enclosed in a laurel wreath. On the lower part of the wreath is a scroll inscribed '*HAMPSHIRE*'. The tiger and wreath are in white metal and the rose and scroll are in gilding metal.

The badge draws on those of two of the units which combined to form the Hampshire Regiment in 1881. It may be expected that the badge would contain some reference to the senior of the two Regular regiments which were brought together under the Cardwell Reforms, but such was not the case. The 37th Foot, which became the 1st Battalion of the new regiment, had no distinguishing badge and it was left to the 67th Foot and the Hampshire Militia to provide the devices on the new badge. The 67th Foot, which became the regiment's 2nd Battalion, had been granted the Royal Tiger for services in India during the period 1805 to 1826, while the Hampshire Rose, in the lower half of the badge, was taken from the Arms of the City of Winchester and had been borne on the Colours and badges of the Hampshire Militia, which subsequently became the 3rd (Militia) Battalion of the Hampshire Regiment.

Eleven battalions of the regiment served in the Second World War, but a number were transferred to other arms and wore the appropriate badges. The remainder wore the above cap-badge, with the exception of the 8th and 11th Battalions (*qv*).

6th (Duke of Connaught's Own) Battalion. This battalion was converted to artillery in 1938 as the 59th Anti-Tank Regiment RA and adopted Royal Artillery cap-badges.

8th (Princess Beatrice's Isle of Wight Rifles) Battalion. Like the 6th Battalion, the 8th was converted to an artillery role in 1937. However, unlike the 6th, it continued to wear its own badge, which is described in Section III.

9th Battalion. The 9th Battalion was formed in 1940 and transferred to the Royal Armoured Corps in November 1941. As the 157th Regiment RAC, it wore the badge and insignia of that corps.

10th Battalion. This battalion, raised the same time as the 9th, was also converted to armour in November 1941, becoming the 147th Regiment RAC. Unlike the 9th, it continued to wear the Hampshire Regiment badge, even though it adopted the black beret of the Royal Armoured Corps.

The Hampshire Regiment
11TH (ROYAL MILITIA, ISLAND OF JERSEY) BATTALION

Upon a saltire, a shield bearing the Arms of Jersey (three lions leoparde in pale) surmounted by an Imperial Crown. The badge is in gilding metal.

The history of the Royal Jersey Militia can be traced back to the Middle Ages, but it was granted the prefix 'Royal' in 1831 to mark the fiftieth anniversary of the defeat of the French invasion of the island in 1781.

The badge incorporates both the Arms of Jersey and the saltire of St Andrew's Cross which is found on the island's flag.

In June 1940 when the British Government ordered the de-militarisation of the Channel Isles, the Commanding Officer of the Royal Jersey Militia requested permission to take the unit to England and on 20 June the entire body of over 200 officers and men embarked on the SS *Holder* for Southampton.

The Militia became the nucleus of the 11th (Royal Militia, Island of Jersey) Battalion of the Hampshire Regiment and Jersey personnel in the battalion were permitted to continue wearing their original cap-badge.

THE SOUTH STAFFORDSHIRE REGIMENT

The Stafford Knot surmounted by an Imperial Crown; below the knot, a scroll inscribed *'SOUTH STAFFORDSHIRE'*. The knot and crown are in white metal and the scroll is in gilding metal.

Badge backing. A Holland Patch (a light brown material) was worn behind the badge. The patch was sanctioned by King George V in 1935 to commemorate the regiment's service in the West Indies during the period 1707–1764.

The Knot is the badge of the Stafford family although it has subsequently been incorporated into the Arms of both the County and Borough of Stafford, as well as being used by both County regiments and the Staffordshire Yeomanry.

The South Staffordshire Regiment was formed in 1881 from the 38th and 80th Regiments of Foot, both of which had had long associations with the county and both of which had incorporated, at various times, the Stafford Knot into their badges. The above badge, however, dates from the amalgamation.

No fewer than fifteen battalions of the regiment were raised during the Second World War and all but four wore the South Staffordshire badge.

Four batalions, the 10th, the 12th, the 13th and 14th, all transferred to the artillery in the period 1941 to 1942 and all adopted the Royal Artillery cap-badge.

The 2nd Battalion, while remaining in an infantry role, became a glider-borne unit in 1942. On doing so, it adopted the maroon beret of the air-borne forces but continued to wear the South Staffordshire badge.

THE DORSETSHIRE REGIMENT

The Castle and key of Gibraltar; above the castle, the sphinx resting upon a tablet inscribed *'MARABOUT'*. Below the castle is a scroll inscribed *'PRIMUS IN INDIS'* (First in India). A laurel wreath encloses the castle and motto and joins the tablet at the top. At the bottom, beneath the first scroll, the laurel wreath joins a second scroll inscribed *'DORSETSHIRE'*. The wreath and the regimental title are in gilding metal, the remainder of the badge is in white metal.

Badge backing. During the later stages of the Second World War, a dark green patch, 2 inches square, representing the facings of the two regiments which together formed the Dorsetshire Regiment, was worn behind the badge by the Regular, Territorial and other active service battalions.

The badge is composed of devices from both the regiments, the 39th and 54th Foot, which were amalgamated in 1881 to form the Dorsetshire Regiment. The 39th Foot (later the 1st Battalion) was honoured by the castle and key of Gibraltar awarded to it for service there during the Great Siege. It was also awarded the motto *'Primus in Indis'* in recognition of it being the first line regiment to see active service in India. The sphinx and the battle-honour 'Marabout' were granted to the 54th Foot (later to become the 2nd Battalion) for service in the Egyptian Campaign of 1801.

Like many county regiments between the wars, the Dorsetshire Regiment had two Regular and two Territorial battalions, but the outbreak of war saw a further five battalions raised. Initially all wore the above badge, although in 1942 two battalions were transferred to the Royal Artillery as Light Anti-Aircraft regiments and adopted artillery badges and insignia.

THE SOUTH LANCASHIRE REGIMENT (THE PRINCE OF WALES'S VOLUNTEERS)

The Prince of Wales's plume, coronet and motto 'ICH DIEN' (I serve). Below, the sphinx resting upon a tablet inscribed 'EGYPT'. Above the Prince of Wales's plume, a scroll inscribed 'SOUTH LANCASHIRE' and below the sphinx and tablet, a scroll inscribed 'PRINCE OF WALES'S VOLUNTEERS'. Branches of laurel connect the ends of the upper and lower scrolls. With the exception of the coronet, the central features of the badge are in white metal; the coronet, the scrolls and laurel are in gilding metal.

Badge backing. A red insert was worn behind the cap-badge. The patch reputedly originated in the Peninsular War and had always been worn by the 2nd Battalion of the 82nd Foot which, in turn, became the 2nd Battalion of the South Lancashire Regiment in 1881. Initially the insert was worn only in the 2nd Battalion, but in 1931 permission was granted for both battalions to wear it.

The regiment was formed by the amalgamation of the 40th and 82nd Regiments of Foot and the above badge draws on the history of both regiments for its composition. The 40th Foot contributed the sphinx which was awarded following action against the French in Egypt during the Napoleonic Wars, while the red backing and the Prince of Wales's badge are derived from the 82nd Foot, whose secondary title was 'The Prince of Wales's Volunteers'.

Although the badge was introduced in 1881, the above title only dates from 1938.

The South Lancashire Regiment raised nine battalions during the Second World War and all but two wore the above badge. The 5th Battalion was transferred to the Royal Artillery while the 2/4th became a battalion of the Parachute Regiment. Each adopted the badge appropriate to its new role.

THE WELCH REGIMENT

The Prince of Wales's plumes, coronet and motto; below, a scroll inscribed '*THE WELCH*'. The feathers and the motto are in white metal while the coronet and scroll are in gilding metal.

The main device of the badge is the emblem of the Prince of Wales which appears on the badge of a number of Welsh regiments and was adopted when the 41st and 69th Regiments of Foot amalgamated to become the Welsh Regiment in 1881. Initially, the cap-badge carried the scroll 'The Welsh', but the 41st had long referred to themselves in the traditional spelling of the word Welch. In 1920, the War Office acceded to a request that this tradition be restored and on 27 January of that year, both the Welch Regiment and the Royal Welch Fusiliers were authorised to wear cap-badges and other appointments with the revised spelling. The old style cap-badge continued in use until existing stocks were expended, which resulted in the changeover being gradual.

The Welch Regiment traced its lineage back to the 1st Regiment of Invalids, raised in 1719. Such units were not uncommon in the eighteenth century and were composed of out-pensioners of Chelsea Hospital who were regarded as too old for active service, but who, nevertheless, were quite capable of performing garrison duties. Personnel of these Regiments of Invalids were not invalids in the modern sense, but simply soldiers who were in receipt of pensions from the Royal Hospital Chelsea.

The regiment was upgraded to a Line regiment in 1787, becoming the 41st Foot. Shortly afterwards it embarked for Canada where it took part in the defeat of the American forces which invaded Ontario during the War of 1812. The regiment returned home at the end of the Napoleonic Wars and assumed its connection with Wales in 1831 when it became the 41st or Welsh

Regiment of Infantry. The 69th Foot, on the other hand, had had no association with the Principality before the amalgamation, being formerly a South Lincolnshire regiment.

During the Second World War the regiment raised nine battalions, all of which, with the exception of the 6th Battalion, wore the Welch Regiment cap-badge.

The 6th Battalion was converted to a searchlight battalion of the Royal Engineers in 1938 and, on transfer to the Royal Artillery in 1940, adopted artillery insignia.

The Welch Regiment saw service in all major theatres of war, the two Regular battalions serving in the Western Desert and the Far East respectively. Two other battalions were engaged in the North West Europe Campaign of 1944–45.

THE BLACK WATCH
(THE ROYAL HIGHLAND REGIMENT)

The Star of the Order of the Thistle, diamond cut; on the star, a thistle wreath; within the wreath an oval inscribed '*NEMO ME IMPUNE LACESSIT*' (No-one provokes me with impunity). Above the oval is an Imperial Crown and within the oval, St Andrew with Cross. Below the wreath is a sphinx on a tablet. The badge is in white metal.

Badge backing. A 3-inch square of Black Watch (or Government) tartan was worn behind the badge on the khaki tam o' shanter, while on the glengarry the badge was backed by a black rosette. On the Balmoral bonnet, a red hackle was usually worn in lieu of the cap-badge.

The Black Watch was formed in 1881 from the 42nd (Royal Highland) Regiment, which became the new regiment's 1st Battalion, and the 73rd (Perthshire) Regiment, but the name and badge reflect the senior of these two regiments.

The 42nd Highlanders, raised in 1739 to assist in the suppression of the Jacobites, was the senior Highland regiment and although it had been known as the Black Watch from shortly after its formation, that title was not officially incorporated into the regiment's designation until 1861. The above title, however, only dated from 1934 when its secondary title was changed – its badge being changed some four years later to the one shown.

The basic design of the badge reflects, through the Star of the Order of the Thistle, the Black Watch's position as the senior Highland regiment, while the sphinx at the base of the oval was awarded to the regiment for its service against the French in the Egyptian Campaign of 1801.

The Black Watch entered the Second World War with six battalions, two Regular and four Territorial. Two battalions, the 1st and 4th, were lost at St Valery in 1940, but were re-formed the same year. Subsequently, four further battalions were raised.

With the exception of the Tyneside Scottish (*qv*), all battalions officially wore the above badge, the pattern of which was sealed in March 1938.

Nevertheless, there is photographic evidence to suggest that badges of the previous design continued to be worn by personnel in the Territorial battalions in the early stages of the war. The main difference, which may be seen from the photograph below, is that the pre-1938 badge had three scrolls: one across the top of the wreath inscribed 'The Royal Highlanders' and two smaller ones at the base bearing the inscription 'Black Watch'.

The pre-1938 badge

The Black Watch
THE TYNESIDE SCOTTISH

St Andrew's Cross, on the lower portion of which is a tablet inscribed 'TYNESIDE SCOTTISH'. Resting on the centre of the cross is a tower surmounted by a Scottish lion bearing in its front paws a flagstaff carrying a swallow-tailed flag in the centre of which is a small St Andrew's Cross. Sprays of thistle emerge from the tablet up each side of the cross. The badge is in white metal.

Badge backing. The badge was backed by a 3-inch square of 42nd, or Government, tartan.

The badge reflects both the Scottish connections of the regiment and its association with Tyneside, for the castle in the centre was taken from the Arms of Newcastle upon Tyne.

The Tyneside Scottish was first raised in October 1914 from Scotsmen living on Tyneside and subsequently four battalions saw active service in the Great War, but the regiment was disbanded shortly after the end of the war. However, on the expansion of the Territorial Army in 1938/39, the 9th Battalion of the Durham Light Infantry was doubled, its duplicate battalion becoming, in October 1939, the 12th (Tyneside Scottish) Battalion, DLI.

In February 1940 the battalion's title was changed yet again to the Tyneside Scottish and on the change it was transferred to the Black Watch, even though throughout the 1940 campaign in Belgium and France over 80 per cent of its personnel were drawn from County Durham.

The regiment returned to France shortly after D-Day but was disbanded in July 1944 after being severely mauled at the Battle of Ravray.

THE OXFORDSHIRE AND BUCKINGHAMSHIRE LIGHT INFANTRY

A bugle with strings, the string tied in three loops. The badge is white metal.

Badge backing. In 1941, the 2nd Battalion was converted to an airborne unit and adopted a maroon beret on which a circular patch (approx 2 inches in diameter) of Light Infantry green was worn behind the cap-badge.

Like all Light Infantry regiments, the Oxfordshire and Buckinghamshire Light Infantry had a strung bugle as its badge, which had been adopted as emblematic of skirmishing or hunting.

The Oxfordshire and Buckinghamshire Light Infantry adopted the above title in 1908 when 'Buckinghamshire' was added to the title of the Oxfordshire Light Infantry and the Rifle Volunteer units of Buckinghamshire became part of the regiment's Territorial component. The Oxfordshire Light Infantry itself was formed in 1881 from the 43rd Monmouthshire Light Infantry and the 52nd Oxfordshire Light Infantry, so that its role as a Light Infantry regiment and its association with Oxfordshire (through the 53rd Light Infantry) pre-date the Cardwell Reforms by some eighty years.

Both the 43rd and 52nd were converted to Light Infantry in 1803 and both served together in the Light Division in the Peninsular War. The 52nd was the first regiment to be designated as Light Infantry and it was because of this seniority that the bugle in its badge had no embellishments.

Eight battalions of the regiment served in the Second World War and all served in an infantry role. With the exception of the two Buckinghamshire battalions (*qv*), all wore the above badge.

The Oxforshire and Buckinghamshire Light Infantry
1ST and 2ND BUCKINGHAMSHIRE BATTALIONS

A Maltese Cross surmounted by an Imperial Crown. On the cross, a circlet inscribed *BUCKINGHAMSHIRE BATTALION*. Within the circle, a swan with a coronet round its neck. The badge is in blackened metal.

Badge backing. The badge was backed by an outline patch of 'Rifle' red.

The Maltese Cross was common to many Rifle regiments and the device of the swan and coronet in the centre of the badge was taken from the Arms of the de Bohun family which were later incorporated into the Arms of Buckinghamshire. The Buckinghamshire battalions traced their descent from the Buckinghamshire Rifle Volunteers, which was raised in 1860, and which, in 1908, became the Buckinghamshire Battalion of the Oxfordshire and Buckinghamshire Light Infantry.

Between the two world wars there was only one battalion in existence, but in April 1939, a second battalion was raised. It, too, wore the above badge. However, the identity of the two battalions was threatened by bureaucrats in the middle of the Second World War and in 1941, Lord Cottesloe, then Lord Lieutenant of the County, had to conduct an extended struggle with the War Office to retain the distinctive badge and titles of the two battalions.

The 1st Battalion served in France and Belgium with the BEF in 1940, before withdrawing through Dunkirk. It returned to France on D-Day as part of No 6 Beach Group, later being designated as a Task Force Battalion and, as such, was involved in attacks on installations of special importance in the Low Countries and Germany.

The 2nd Battalion served on home defence duties until July 1944 when it was disbanded.

THE ESSEX REGIMENT

The Castle of Gibraltar with a key depending from the base; above the castle the Sphinx on a tablet inscribed 'EGYPT'; the whole, with the exception of the sphinx, enclosed in an oak wreath. On the lower portion of the wreath is a scroll inscribed 'THE ESSEX REGIMENT'. The castle and wreath are in gilding metal and the sphinx and scroll are in white metal.

Badge backing. From 1943, the badge was backed by a patch of 'Pompadour' purple, the colour being taken from the facings of the 56th Foot and, reputedly, the favourite colour of Madame de Pompadour. The shape of the patch varied according to the battalion: for example, the 1st Battalion wore a diamond patch, while that of the 2nd Battalion was circular.

The Essex Regiment was formed in 1881 from the former 44th (East Essex) and 56th (West Essex) Regiments, so its connection with its county, unlike many other regiments, pre-dates the Cardwell Reforms. Its badge records battle-honours awarded to both regiments. From the 44th Foot it took the sphinx, awarded for service during the Egyptian Campaign of 1801, and from the 56th the representation of the castle and key of Gibraltar which was granted to the regiment in recognition of its participation in the defence of Gibraltar during the Great Siege.

Eleven battalions of the Essex Regiment served in the Second World War, but only five served in an infantry role. Of the six which transferred to other arms, the following continued to wear the above badge:

1/6th Battalion. The 1/6th Battalion was transferred to the Royal Artillery as the 64th Searchlight Regiment RA in 1940.

2/6th Battalion. A duplicate of the 6th Battalion, the 2/6th also became a searchlight regiment.

7th Battalion. The 7th Battalion was converted to an anti-aircraft role and was transferred to the Royal Artillery as early as 1935 and so was no longer a constituent part of the regiment by the outbreak of war. Nonetheless, it, too, continued to wear the Essex badge.

8th Battalion. The 8th Battalion converted to armour in 1941, becoming the 153rd Regiment, Royal Armoured Corps.

The two battalions which adopted the badges of their new regiments were:

9th Battalion. The 9th Battalion transferred to artillery in 1942 as the 11th (Essex) Medium Regiment RA and subsequently wore Royal Artillery insignia.

10th Battalion. On the formation of the Parachute Regiment in 1942, the 10th Battalion was re-designated as the 9th Battalion of the new regiment and adopted its badge.

THE SHERWOOD FORESTERS (NOTTINGHAMSHIRE AND DERBYSHIRE REGIMENT)

A Maltese Cross surmounted by an Imperial Crown; in the centre of the cross a wreath of oak and within the wreath a stag, lodged on the left arm of the cross and across the left branch of the wreath, a straight scroll inscribed '*SHERWOOD*'; on the right arm of the cross and on the right branch of the wreath, a straight scroll inscribed '*FORESTERS*'. Below the cross a scroll inscribed '*NOTTS AND DERBY*'. The badge is in white metal except for the lower scroll, which is in gilding metal.

Badge backing. A square patch of Lincoln Green was worn behind the badge of most battalions. The 6th Battalion, however, wore its patch in the form of a diamond.

The regiment was formed in 1881 from the former 45th (Nottinghamshire) and the 95th (Derbyshire) Regiments of Foot and it is from the latter that the main devices of the badge: the Maltese Cross, the oak wreath and the stag were taken. The adoption of the badge was unusual in that the Derbyshire Regiment was the junior of the two regiments and consequently became the 2nd Battalion of the Sherwood Foresters. Furthermore, for the first twenty-seven years of the regiment's existence, the scroll beneath the badge simply bore the inscription 'Derbyshire'. It was not until 1908 that the above badge was adopted with a new scroll which acknowledged both Nottinghamshire and Derbyshire.

Fourteen battalions of the Sherwood Foresters served at various times in the Second World War, excluding the 6th and 7th Battalions, both of which had been transferred to the Royal Engineers in 1936.

However, several battalions changed both their numbering and their roles in the period 1939–45, with consequent changes to their badges and other insignia.

2/5th Battalion. The 2/5th Battalion was raised as a duplicate of the 5th on the expansion of the Territorial Army in 1939, the 5th Battalion then being re-numbered 1/5th. The 1/5th was subsequently lost in the Fall of Singapore in January 1942 and in the following year the 2/5th was re-designated the 5th Battalion.

6th Battalion. Although converted to Royal Engineers in 1936 as the 40th (Sherwood Foresters) Anti-Aircraft Battalion, it continued to wear the Sherwood Foresters badge. On transfer to the Royal Artillery in 1940, the battalion adopted artillery insignia.

7th (Robin Hoods) Battalion. Like the 6th Battalion, the 7th was converted to a searchlight unit in 1936, becoming the 42nd Anti-Aircraft Battalion RE, and on doing so adopted a Royal Engineers' badge. In 1940, on transfer to the Royal Artillery, it re-adopted its former badge, details of which appear in Section III.

9th Battalion. Converted to armour in 1941 as the 112th Regiment, the Royal Armoured Corps, the 9th Battalion continued to wear the Sherwood Foresters' badge until it was disbanded in 1944.

13th Battalion. Although it served in armour as the 163rd Regiment RAC during 1942 and 1943, the 13th Battalion then reverted to an infantry role. However, even during the period in the Royal Armoured Corps it continued to wear its regimental cap-badge.

THE LOYAL REGIMENT (NORTH LANCASHIRE)

The Royal Crest (i.e. the Lion upon the Crown); below the crown a rose and below the rose, a scroll inscribed 'THE LOYAL REGIMENT'. The Royal Crest is in white metal while the rose and scroll are in gilding metal.

The Royal Crest and rose which figure prominently in the badge both refer to the regiment's Lancastrian connections. The Crest is that of the Duchy of Lancaster, a Royal Dukedom, and the rose represents the Red Rose of Lancaster. Of the Loyal Regiment's antecedents only one, the 47th Foot, had a Lancashire background; the 2nd Battalion, the former 81st Foot, originated in Lincolnshire as the Loyal Lincoln Volunteers. It was from the latter that the regiment adopted its title, although it was not until 1920 that the above designation was officially accepted.

During the Second World War ten battalions were raised, but only a minority actually continued to wear the regimental badge, the remainder being transferred to other arms.

4th Battalion. Originally converted to a searchlight regiment in the Royal Engineers it was subsequently transferred to the Royal Artillery as the 150th Light Anti-Aircraft Regiment RA in 1940 and adopted artillery insignia.

5th Battalion. On the formation of the Reconnaissance Corps in 1941, the 5th Battalion became the 18th (Loyal North Lancashire) Regiment of the Corps and wore its badges.

6th Battalion. The 6th Battalion was also transferred to the Reconnaissance Corps and it, too, wore Reconnaissance Corps badges.

7th and 8th Battalions. Both these battalions were transferred to the Royal Artillery as the 92nd and 93rd Light Anti-Aircraft Regiments RA and wore artillery badges.

THE NORTHAMPTONSHIRE REGIMENT

The Castle and key of Gibraltar within a laurel wreath; above the castle is a scroll inscribed *'GIBRALTAR'* and below the castle another scroll inscribed *'TALAVERA'*. On the lower part of the wreath is a scroll inscribed *'NORTHAMPTONSHIRE'*. The badge is in white metal with the exception of the regimental title which is in gilding metal.

Badge backing. A circular black patch was worn behind the badge when worn in the cap GS. A black patch had originally been introduced behind the badge in the Boer War, the colour being taken from the coat of arms of the founding colonel of the 48th Foot.

The Northamptonshire Regiment was formed from the former 48th (Northamptonshire) and 58th (Rutlandshire) Regiments of Foot. It is from the latter, which became the 2nd Battalion of the new regiment, that the main device of the badge, the Castle of Gibraltar, was taken; the 58th Foot having been awarded the battle-honour for its part in the siege of 1779–83. The battle-honour 'Talavera' had been awarded to the 48th Foot in recognition of that regiment's outstanding service during the Peninsular War, particularly at the Battle of Talavera itself in 1809.

Until 1938, the Northamptonshire Regiment consisted of four battalions, two Regular and two Territorial (the 4th and the 5th), but in that year the 4th Battalion transferred to the Royal Engineers as the 50th Anti-Aircraft Battalion, RE and no longer wore the Northamptonshire badge. However, following the expansion of the Territorial Army in 1939, a new 4th Battalion was raised. A further three battalions were subsequently raised, and all served in an infantry role and wore the above cap-badge.

THE ROYAL BERKSHIRE REGIMENT
(PRINCESS CHARLOTTE OF WALES'S)

A Chinese dragon above a scroll inscribed 'ROYAL BERKSHIRE'. The badge is in gilding metal.

Badge backing. A triangular red patch pointing downwards was worn behind the badge when worn in the cap GS. In the field service cap, the red backing was trimmed to the shape of the badge.

The Chinese dragon in the regiment's badge was awarded to the 49th Foot, which was to become the 1st Battalion of the Royal Berkshire Regiment, for its service in China during the Opium War of 1840–42. The triangular patch behind the badge was also taken from the 49th Foot and recalled an incident when the Light Company of the regiment carried out a daring night attack on the American colonists during the Baffle of Brandywine in the American War of Independence.

The 49th Foot was linked with the 66th in 1881 to form Princess Charlotte of Wales's (Berkshire Regiment) and although the 49th was the senior, it was the 66th Foot, which became the new regiment's 2nd Battalion, which had had a previous territorial connection with the county, having had 'Berkshire' added to its title as early as 1782. The regiment was granted the prefix 'Royal' following service in the Sudan in 1885 and adopted the above title in 1920.

During the Second World War, the Royal Berkshire Regiment raised ten battalions including the 5th (Hackney) and 7th (Stoke Newington) Battalions which had been transferred to the London Regiment in 1937. All regiments wore the above badge and none was transferred to any other arm.

THE QUEEN'S OWN ROYAL WEST KENT REGIMENT

The White Horse of Kent standing on a scroll inscribed '*INVICTA*' (Unconquered) in Old English lettering. Below the motto-scroll is a second scroll inscribed '*ROYAL WEST KENT*'. The badge is in white metal.

The regiment was formed in 1881 from the 50th and 97th Regiments of Foot. The 50th Foot, which became the 1st Battalion of the new regiment, had been associated with West Kent since 1782 and had been granted the title 'The Queen's Own' in 1831 on the accession of King William IV, to whose consort the title refers.

The regiment took its badge from the Arms of the County of Kent, arms which had also been borne by the former Kent Militia.

During the Second World War, the regiment raised five battalions in addition to the two Regular battalions. However, the 9th and 10th Battalions were converted to artillery regiments in 1941 and adopted the cap-badge and other insignia of the Royal Artillery.

Battalions of the Queen's Own Royal West Kent Regiment served in all major theatres of war, including North West Europe, Africa, Italy and Burma. It was during the latter campaign that a member of the 4th Battalion won the VC at Kohima.

THE KING'S OWN YORKSHIRE LIGHT INFANTRY

A French horn with a rose in the centre. The badge is in white metal.

Badge backing. A rectangular patch of Light Infantry green was worn behind the badge when worn in the cap GS.

The French horn is a form of bugle which is associated with all Light Infantry regiments, while the rose in the centre of the horn represented the White Rose of York.

The King's Own Yorkshire Light Infantry traced its Light Infantry origins to both its constituent regiments: the 51st Regiment, from which the 1st Battalion had been formed, became a Light Infantry corps in 1809, while the 2nd Battalion had been the 105th Madras Light Infantry, one of the European regiments originally raised in British India by the East India Company.

Although, obviously, the 2nd Battalion had no previous connection with Yorkshire, the 51st Foot had had been associated with the county since 1809, when it was given the secondary title of the 2nd Yorkshire, West Riding Regiment.

Nine battalions were raised during the Second World War of which three were transferred to other arms and wore the cap-badges indicated. Otherwise all battalions wore the above badge.

5th Battalion. The 5th Battalion became the 53rd Light Anti-Aircraft Regiment RA in 1938 and subsequently wore Royal Artillery badges.

7th Battalion. Formed in July 1940, the 7th Battalion converted to armour in October 1941 as the 149th Regiment RAC and wore Royal Armoured Corps badges.

THE KING'S SHROPSHIRE LIGHT INFANTRY

A strung bugle-horn, the strings tied in three bows. Within the bend of the bugle and below the strings, the letters 'KSLI' between bars. The bugle and strings are in white metal and the lettering is in gilding metal.

Badge backing. Some battalions wore a patch of Light Infantry green behind their badges, but the shape of the patch depended upon the battalion:

1st Battalion. In the 1st Battalion, the backing to the badge was in the shape of the outline of the badge itself. In addition, a band of green was worn round the base of the cap GS.
2nd Battalion. A circular patch was worn behind the badge.
4th Battalion. The third of the battalions to wear a green backing to the cap-badge, the 4th Battalion opted for a rectangular patch.

The King's Shropshire Light Infantry was descended from the 53rd Foot, which had been associated with Shropshire since 1782, and the 85th, which had been designated Light Infantry in 1808 and granted the title 'The King's' on the accession of King William IV in 1821. Like all Light Infantry regiments the main device of its badge was the bugle, but the above title and badge were not adopted in 1920.

Eight battalions of the regiment served in the Second World War and all initially served in an infantry role. However, in 1942 the 6th and 7th Battalions were transferred to the Royal Artillery in 1942 as the 181st Field and 99th Anti-Tank Regiments respectively. On transfer both adopted Royal Artillery badges.

The King's Shropshire Light Infantry
THE HEREFORDSHIRE REGIMENT

A lion passant guardant, holding in the dexter paw and standing on a straight wreath, all on a scroll inscribed '*HEREFORDSHIRE*'. The lion and sword are in white metal and the scroll is in gilding metal.

Badge backing. In the 1st Battalion, the badge was backed by a 2-inch green square. The reason for the choice of colour of the backing is unclear. It may have been to associate the regiment more closely with its parent corps, the KSLI, or because the 36th Foot (The Herefordshire Regiment) had grass green facings on its uniform. There was, however, no lineal connection between the 36th Foot, which became the 2nd Battalion of the Worcestershire Regiment in 1881, and the Herefordshire Regiment, which was formed in 1908. The shade of green in the backing varied considerably and certainly the members of one draft which joined the regiment during the North West Europe Campaign were issued with backing which had been 'liberated' from the billiard table of a bar in the Netherlands!

The 2nd Battalion adopted a red rectangular patch although, again, there was no historic reason for the choice.

The Herefordshire Regiment was originally formed from a number of rifle volunteer units which, in 1881, became the 4th (Herefordshire Militia) Battalion of the King's Shropshire Light Infantry. On the formation of the Territorial Force, however, it became one of the four 'regiments' of infantry in that force, although it still retained its association with the KSLI.

The badge of the regiment is taken from the Arms of the City of Hereford.

The Herefordshire Regiment maintained one battalion until 1939, when a duplicate battalion was raised. The 1st Battalion served in the 159th Brigade, seeing service in North West Europe from Normandy to the Baltic. The 2nd Battalion remained as a home defence battalion.

THE MIDDLESEX REGIMENT
(THE DUKE OF CAMBRIDGE'S OWN)

The Prince of Wales's plume, coronet and motto '*ICH DIEN*' on a scroll; below the scroll, the coronet and cypher of HRH The Duke of Cambridge interlaced and reversed, all within a laurel wreath. Across the bottom of the scroll is a wreath inscribed '*ALBUHERA*' and below the wreath another scroll inscribed '*MIDDLESEX REGIMENT*'. The plume, motto and title scroll are in white metal and the remainder of the badge is in gilding metal.

Badge backing. A diamond in the regimental colours of gold-yellow and dark maroon was worn behind the badge, the maroon being worn on the right-hand side of the diamond. This backing was first adopted in the First World War when the regiment expanded to over forty battalions. It dropped out of use between the wars, but was re-introduced in 1939. The origins of the patch reflect the colours of the two regiments which combined to form the Middlesex Regiment in 1881.

The above badge also owes its origin to the two constituent regiments. The cypher and ducal coronet were derived from the 77th (East Middlesex) Regiment, which had been granted the title of the Duke of Cambridge's Own in 1876; the battle-honour 'Albuhera' was that of the 57th (West Middlesex) Regiment, which also gave the regiment its nickname of 'The Diehards'.

No fewer than thirteen battalions of the Middlesex Regiment served in the Second World War and all wore the above cap-badge. Even the 9th Battalion, which was transferred to the Royal Artillery as the 60th Searchlight Regiment RA, continued to do so.

In 1942, the 2/8th Battalion was re-numbered, following the loss of the 1st Battalion in the fall of Hong Kong.

The Middlesex Regiment
(The Duke of Cambridge's Own)
PRINCESS LOUISE'S KENSINGTON REGIMENT

The Arms of the Royal Borough of Kensington on an eight-pointed star. The arms consist of a shield quartered within a quartered border. In the first quarter of the shield is a celestial crown above a fleur-de-lys; in the second quarter a cross flory and four martlets; in the third a cross bottony and four roses while in the fourth quarter there is a mitre. The badge is in either white or gilding metal.

Princess Louise's Kensington Regiment was raised, as were many of the London regiments, in 1859 at the time of a threatened invasion by Napoleon III. Its original title was the 4th Middlesex Rifle Volunteers, but on the formation of the London Regiment in 1908, it became that regiment's 13th Battalion. In 1922 it became the 13th London Regiment, with the secondary title of Princess Louise's Kensington Regiment. However, on the disbandment of the London Regiment in 1937, the unit was transferred back to the corps of the Middlesex Regiment.

The badge, which was based on the Arms of the Royal Borough of Kensington, was adopted in 1908 on the formation of the London Regiment.

During the period between the wars the regiment maintained one battalion, but in 1938 a second battalion was raised and both served in an infantry role in the Second World War.

Both battalions wore the above badge.

THE KING'S ROYAL RIFLE CORPS

A Maltese Cross, on the top arm of which is a tablet inscribed '*CELER ET AUDAX*' (swift and bold). Above the tablet is an Imperial Crown. In the centre of the cross, a circle inscribed '*THE KING'S ROYAL RIFLE CORPS*'. Within the circle is a bugle with strings, and battle-honours are inscribed on each arm of the cross. The badge is in blackened metal.

Badge backing. The badge was outlined with a patch of Rifle red.

The regiment was raised in 1755 as the 62nd Foot, but in 1757 it became the 60th Royal American Regiment. It was for service in North America under General Wolfe that the regiment was granted the motto '*Celer et Audax*'. By 1824 it had became a Rifle Corps, hence the bugle in the centre of the badge; the Maltese Cross is also common to Rifle regiments – possibly as a means of displaying battle-honours in lieu of colours.

The above title was not adopted until 1881, when the circle at the centre of the cross was so inscribed.

On the disbanding of the London Regiment in 1937, three of its constituent battalions: Queen Victoria's Rifles, the Rangers and the Queen's Westminsters, were transferred to the King's Royal Rifle Corps as its Territorial component.

On the doubling up of the Territorial Army in 1938, each of the above regiments raised a second battalion, so that the KRRC entered the war with two Regular and six Territorial battalions. These Territorial units retained their individual identities until 1941 when they formally became battalions of their parent regiment and adopted the badge of the King's Royal Rifle Corps.

The exception was the 1st Battalion of the Queen Victoria's Rifles, which, together with the 2nd Battalion of the KRRC, was lost in the defence of Calais in 1940. Both battalions were reformed in the same year, and from the date of its re-formation the Queen Victoria's Rifles adopted a King's Royal Rifle Corps badge, although it did not officially become the regiment's 7th Battalion until, as has been stated, 1941.

The King's Royal Rifle Corps
QUEEN VICTORIA'S RIFLES

A Maltese Cross with a circlet in the centre inscribed '*QUEEN VICTORIA'S RIFLES*' enclosing St George and the Dragon. Above the cross is a tablet inscribed '*SOUTH AFRICA 1900–02*' surmounted by an Imperial Crown. The badge is in blackened brass or white metal.

Queen Victoria's Rifles traced its origins back to the 1st and 11th Middlesex Rifle Volunteers which were raised, as were many of the Volunteer Rifle Corps, to counter the threat of a French invasion in the mid-nineteenth century. However, the two units were amalgamated in 1892 and it was from the 1st (the Victoria Volunteer Rifle Corps) that the regiment took its title and from the 11th (St George's Volunteer Rifle Corps) that it took the device in the centre of the cross. The final element of the badge, the battle-honour 'South Africa', was awarded for service in the Second Boer War.

The regiment became a Volunteer battalion of the King's Royal Rifle Corps at the time of the amalgamation, but it was transferred to the London Regiment as its 9th Battalion on the formation of the latter regiment in 1908. After two changes of title, it assumed the above title and badge when it re-joined the corps of the KRRC in 1937.

A second battalion of the Queen Victoria's Rifles was raised on the expansion of the Territorial Army in 1938, but both battalions were formally transferred to their parent regiment as its 7th and 8th Battalions in 1941.

The 1st Battalion had already adopted the KRRC cap-badge in 1940, prior to becoming its 7th Battalion, but the 2nd Battalion did not follow suit until officially incorporated.

The King's Royal Rifle Corps
THE RANGERS

A Maltese Cross in the centre of which is a circlet inscribed *'THE KING'S ROYAL RIFLE CORPS'* enclosing a strung bugle. Above the top arm of the cross is an Imperial Crown. Battle-honours are inscribed on all four arms of the badge. Below the cross is a scroll inscribed *'THE RANGERS'*. The badge is in blackened brass.

A descendant of yet another of the London rifle volunteer corps of the mid-nineteenth century, the Rangers began its existence as the 40th Middlesex Rifle Volunteers. The regiment was incorporated into the London Regiment as its 12th Battalion in 1908, but was transferred to the King's Royal Rifle Corps in 1937 on the disbandment of the London Regiment.

The above badge was adopted on transfer and was very similar to that of its parent regiment, although it did not have the red cloth backing.

Two battalions of the Rangers served in the Second World War and while the 2nd Battalion remained in the United Kingdom as a training unit, the 1st Battalion saw active service in the Western Desert, Greece and Crete in 1941. The battalion was almost wiped out in the latter campaign, but was subsequently re-formed in Egypt.

In the same year, the two battalions were re-numbered as the 9th and 10th Battalions of the King's Royal Rifle Corps and no longer wore the Rangers badge. In any event, the 10th did not long survive the change of name, being disbanded in August 1942.

The King's Royal Rifle Corps
THE QUEEN'S WESTMINSTERS

A Maltese Cross surmounted by an Imperial Crown; battle-honours are inscribed on all four arms of the cross. In the centre of the cross are two oval escutcheons, the left one bearing a portcullis – the Arms of Westminster – and the right hand one, which overlaps the left, bearing the Prince of Wales's plume and coronet. The badge is in blackened brass.

The Queen's Westminsters was formed in 1921 from the 15th and 16th Battalions of the London Regiment. The 15th Battalion had formerly been the Civil Service Rifles and it was from this unit that the escutcheon with the Prince of Wales's badge was taken; King Edward VII and King Edward VIII each having been Honorary Colonels of the regiment while they were Prince of Wales. The 16th Battalion, formerly the 22nd Middlesex Rifle Volunteers, was raised in Westminster, hence the badge on the left hand escutcheon.

Although the Queen's Westminsters became part of the corps of the KRRC on the disbanding of the London Regiment in 1937, it continued to wear the above badge which had been adopted at the time of its formation.

A second battalion of the regiment was raised prior to the outbreak of war and the two battalions continued to retain their own identity until 1941 when they became the 11th and 12th Battalions of their parent regiment and adopted the cap-badge of the King's Royal Rifle Corps.

THE WILTSHIRE REGIMENT
(THE DUKE OF EDINBURGH'S)

A cross pattee in the centre of which is the monogram 'AEA', interlaced and reversed. The cross is surmounted by a ducal coronet and below the cross is a scroll inscribed 'THE WILTSHIRE REGIMENT'. The badge is in gilding metal.

Badge backing. In the 2nd and 4th Battalions the badge was backed by a maroon patch, 2 inches square, while the 5th Battalion wore a blue square. The maroon patch was derived from the regimental colour of the 62nd (Wiltshire) Regiment although there appears to be no reason for the colour of the square adopted by the 5th Battalion.

The coronet and monogram AEA are those of Alfred Ernest Albert, Duke of Edinburgh, the second son of Queen Victoria.

The Wiltshire Regiment was formed from the 62nd and 99th Regiments of Foot, the 62nd having been associated with Wiltshire since 1782. It is, however, from the 99th Foot, which became the regiment's 2nd Battalion, that the main device of the badge was taken. The 99th Foot had been granted the secondary title of the 'Duke of Edinburgh's' in 1874, just seven years before the amalgamation, and brought with it the recognition of a royal connection in the shape of the cross and coronet.

During 1939–45 the regiment raised six battalions, all of which served in an infantry role.

Whilst the 1st Battalion spent the whole of the war in the Far East, the 2nd Battalion served in places as far apart as Dunkirk, Madagascar, India and Italy, before joining the 4th and 5th Battalions in North West Europe in 1944.

THE MANCHESTER REGIMENT

A fleur-de-lys. The badge is in brass.

The fleur-de-lys was probably adopted by the 63rd Regiment in 1815 to commemorate its service in the former French island of Guadeloupe. However, on the formation of the Manchester Regiment from the 63rd and 96th Regiments in 1881, the fleur-de-lys was superseded by the coat of arms of the City of Manchester. This badge was never popular, being referred to as the 'Tram Conductor's badge', and in 1923 the fleur-de-lys was re-adopted by the regiment.

In addition to the two Regular battalions, a further ten Territorial and war-service battalions of the Manchester Regiment served in the Second World War. With the exception of the following, all the battalions served in an infantry role and all wore the above badge:

5th Battalion. Returning to England after the fall of France in 1940, the 5th Battalion was reformed as the 111th Regiment, Royal Armoured Corps and wore RAC badges. In 1943, it was converted back to infantry and again wore the Manchester Regiment badge.

6th Battalion. The original 6th/7th Battalion was converted to artillery in 1936 and adopted Royal Artillery badges, but a new 6th Battalion was formed in 1939 and remained in an infantry role throughout the war.

9th Battalion. The 9th Battalion doubled up in 1939 to form the 1/9th and 2/9th Battalions, both of which were initially machine-gun units. However, in 1940 the 2/9th was transferred to the Royal Artillery as the 88th Anti-Tank Regiment RA and adopted artillery insignia.

10th Battalion. The 10th Battalion was converted to armour in 1939 becoming the 41st (Oldham) Regiment RTR and, as such, wore Royal Tank Regiment badges.

THE NORTH STAFFORDSHIRE REGIMENT (THE PRINCE OF WALES'S)

The Stafford Knot with the Prince of Wales's plume, coronet and motto (*Ich Dien*) above: below the knot, a scroll inscribed '*NORTH STAFFORD*'. The knot and coronet are in gilding metal and the remainder of the badge is white metal.

The North Staffordshire Regiment was formed in 1881 from the former 64th Foot (or 2nd Staffordshire Regiment) and the 98th Foot, which had been granted, in 1876, the secondary title of the 'Prince of Wales's'.

Like that of the other Staffordshire regiments, the main device in the badge of the North Staffordshire Regiment was the Stafford Knot which it inherited from the 64th Foot. From the 98th, it took the Prince of Wales's plume and coronet.

During the Second World War, four battalions, in addition to the two Regular and two Territorial battalions, were raised, and no variations to the badge were worn.

However, in January 1942 two battalions, the 8th and the 9th, were transferred to other arms. The 8th became a Royal Artillery regiment, while the 9th joined the Royal Armoured Corps. On conversion, each adopted the badge of the receiving formation.

THE YORK AND LANCASTER REGIMENT

The Royal Tiger with the Union Rose above and a ducal coronet above the rose; the tiger is within a scroll inscribed *'YORK AND LANCASTER'*. A laurel wreath continues from each arm of the scroll, meeting at the lower point of the coronet. The badge is in gilding metal, except for the coronet and the outer petals of the rose.

The main two devices of the badge of the York and Lancaster Regiment were the Royal Tiger and the Union Rose, each representing one of the regiments which combined to form the new regiment in 1881. The Royal Tiger had been granted as a badge to the 65th Foot in recognition of its service in India. The other constituent regiment, the 84th Foot, had been granted the secondary title of 'The York and Lancaster' in 1809 and adopted the Union Rose soon afterwards to represent its connection with the two counties. Similarly, the ducal coronet can be ascribed to the regiment's association with the two royal dukedoms of York and Lancaster. Despite its title, the York and Lancaster Regiment was recruited almost entirely from the West Riding of Yorkshire.

Ten battalions of the York and Lancaster Regiment served in the Second World War, although two were converted to other arms.

5th Battalion. The 5th Bn was converted to artillery as the 27th (York and Lancaster) Heavy Artillery Regiment in 1936 and Royal Artillery cap-badges were worn.

10th Battalion. On conversion to armour in 1940 when the battalion became the 150th Regiment RAC, it ceased to wear the regimental cap-badge. However, although the unit remained in the RAC, its regimental cap-badge was restored in 1944.

THE DURHAM LIGHT INFANTRY

A bugle with strings taken upwards into a crown: within the strings the letters '*DLI*'. The bugle is ornamented with a leaf motif. The whole badge is in white metal.

Badge backing. The badge was backed by a patch of Light Infantry green. The shape of the patch varied, depending upon the battalion, for while the 1st Battalion adopted a 2-inch square, most other battalions wore a circular patch.

The bugle forming the badge of the Durham Light Infantry was common to all Light Infantry regiments. The 68th Foot, which later became the 1st Battalion of the DLI, had been created a Light Infantry regiment in 1808, but its association with County Durham extended back to 1792. In 1881 it was united with the 106th Foot, formerly the 2nd Bombay Light Infantry, when the above title and badge were adopted.

No fewer than eighteen battalions of the regiment served in the Second World War and, of these, twelve saw service overseas in all major theatres of war. Not all, however, served in an infantry role and of those which did, two wore different badges from that shown above. The following battalions were either transferred to other arms or wore a different badge:

5th Battalion. In 1938 the battalion was expanded to form the 1/5th DLI (54th Searchlight Battalion RE) and the 2/5th DLI (55th Searchlight Regiment RE), but both battalions continued to wear the badge of their parent regiment. In 1940 both battalions were transferred to the Royal Artillery as the 54th Searchlight Regiment (DLI) and the 113rd Light Anti-Aircraft Regiment (DLI) respectively. Royal Artillery badges were worn, but a backing of Light Infantry green was worn behind the RA "bomb" badge in the Field Service and General Service caps.

6th Battalion. The 6th Battalion (*qv*) continued to wear its own blackened badge to denote its Rifle volunteer origins.

7th Battalion. Transferred to the Royal Engineers in 1936 as the 47th (DLI) Anti-Aircraft Battalion, the battalion continued to wear the cap-badge of the DLI. In 1940, it was transferred to the Royal Artillery as the 112th Light Anti-Aircraft Regiment (DLI) and adopted Royal Artillery cap-badges. Like the 1/5th and 2/5th Battalions, the 7th continued to recall its association with its parent regiment through a green backing to its cap-badge.

12th Battalion. Originally formed as a duplicate of the 9th Battalion on the expansion of the Territorial Army, the 12th Battalion changed its name to the Tyneside Scottish (*qv*) and was subsequently transferred to the corps of the Black Watch in February 1940.

15th Battalion. Raised in 1940, in 1942 the battalion was converted to armour as the 155th Regiment (15th DLI) RAC. While the rest of the battalion adopted the badge of the Royal Armoured Corps, the band and bugles of the battalion continued to wear the badge and other appointments of their parent regiment. In addition, the DLI cap-badge continued to be worn by all ranks in the Field Service cap for 'walking out'.

While the Regular battalions of the DLI were involved in the Far East and Eastern Mediterranean, the majority of the Territorial and war-service battalions saw service with the BEF in 1940 and, as part of 50th (Northumbrian) Division, in the Middle East, Italy and back to North West Europe, where, at one time, no fewer than five battalions were together in the line.

The Durham Light Infantry
6TH BATTALION

A bugle with strings taken upwards into an Imperial Crown; within the strings, the letters *'DLI'*. The bugle is ornamented with a leaf motif. The badge is in blackened metal.

Badge backing. When the cap GS was worn, the badge was backed by a 2-inch square of Rifle red.

The 6th Battalion of the Durham Light Infantry traced its origins back to the 21st Durham (Barnard Castle) Rifle Volunteers of the mid-nineteenth century, which, in 1887, became the 2nd Volunteer Battalion of the DLI. On the formation of the Territorial Force in 1908 it became the 6th Battalion of the Durham Light Infantry and was alone among the formations incorporated into the county regiment which refused to surrender its Rifle Volunteer traditions. It was perhaps not insignificant that the Colonel of the battalion was, at that time, the Lord Lieutenant of the County and thus while other volunteer units were obliged to conform, the 6th, through his patronage, was able to retain its identity.

As a result, personnel in the battalion continued to wear blackened badges and wore the battalion's battle-honours on their belts instead of on Regimental colours.

With the expansion of the Territorial Army in 1938 a duplicate battalion of the 6th, initially the 2/6th, but later re-numbered the 10th Battalion, was formed, but, unlike its progenitor, it adopted neither the blackened badge nor other insignia of a Rifle unit.

In common with other Territorial battalions of the DLI, the 6th formed part of the 50th (Northumbrian) Division and served in the Western Desert, Italy and back to North West Europe, where it had served with the BEF in 1939–40.

THE HIGHLAND LIGHT INFANTRY (CITY OF GLASGOW REGIMENT)

The Star of the Order of the Thistle and thereon a bugle-horn. In the twist of the bugle, the monogram '*HLI*'. Above the horn, an Imperial Crown and below, a scroll inscribed '*ASSAYE*'. Below the scroll is an elephant. The badge is in white metal.

Badge backing. The regiment wore a Mackenzie tartan patch as backing to the badge.

The badge was based on the Order of the Thistle, a device common to a number of other Scottish regiments. The bugle, the distinguishing badge of all Light Infantry regiments, was drawn from the 71st Foot which had been re-titled the Highland Light Infantry when it became a Light Infantry corps in 1809. The elephant and the battle-honour 'Assaye' allude to the contribution to the Battle of Assaye in 1803 by the 74th Highlanders which, in 1881, became the 2nd Battalion of the HLI.

Although the badge dated from 1881, the above name was of more recent origin, the secondary title of 'The City of Glasgow Regiment' not being added until 1923.

During the Second World War, the Highland Light Infantry raised twelve battalions and all wore the HLI cap-badge except the 9th which, in 1938, became the 1st Battalion, the Glasgow Highlanders and adopted its own badge (*qv*). Nonetheless, the Glasgow Highlanders continued to remain part of the corps of the Highland Light Infantry.

Even the two battalions that transferred to other arms: the 7th, which became the 88th Anti-Aircraft Regiment RA, and the 11th, which became the 156th Regiment, Royal Armoured Corps, continued to wear the HLI cap-badge.

The Highland Light Infantry
THE GLASGOW HIGHLANDERS

The Star of the Order of the Thistle. On the Star, a thistle wreath enclosing an oval inscribed 'NEMO ME IMPUNE LACESSIT' (no-one provokes me with impunity) and surmounted by an Imperial Crown. Within the oval, St Andrew and Cross. Across the top of the wreath is a two-part scroll inscribed 'THE GLASGOW HIGHLANDERS' and a similar three-part scroll at the base inscribed 'HIGHLAND LIGHT INFANTRY'. The whole badge is in white metal.

Badge backing. Unlike its parent regiment, the HLI, the Glasgow Highlanders wore a patch of Government tartan behind its cap-badge. Its pipers, too, differed and wore a Royal Stuart patch.

The Glasgow Highlanders traced its origins back to the nineteenth century when, as the 105th Lanarkshire (Glasgow Highland) Rifle Volunteers, it was raised, during the threat of a French invasion, from Highlanders living in Glasgow. From the start the unit was kilted, its uniform similar to the Black Watch from which it took the basis of its badge. Indeed, with the cavalier attitude typical of the Rifle Volunteers in general, and with a fine disregard for tradition, the Lanarkshire Rifle Volunteers even adopted the battle-honour of the 42nd Highlanders which had been awarded to that regiment for service in Egypt in the Napoleonic Wars.

It became part of the Highland Light Infantry in 1887 as the regiment's 5th (Glasgow Highland) Volunteer Battalion, but retained both its badge and the Government tartan. In 1908, on the establishment of the Territorial Force, it became the 9th (Glasgow Highland) Battalion of the HLI. However, its common title remained, as it had been for many years: the Glasgow Highlanders. It was, as the Regimental History of the HLI suggests, virtually a regiment within a regiment.

In 1939, on the raising of a duplicate battalion, the 2/9th, authorisation was given to adopt the title 'The Glasgow Highlanders (Highland Light Infantry)' and the two battalions became the 1st and 2nd respectively of the new regiment, keeping both the distinctive badge and tartan.

THE SEAFORTH HIGHLANDERS
(THE ROSS-SHIRE BUFFS, THE DUKE OF ALBANY'S)

A stag's head caboshed (cut to show no neck) above a scroll inscribed '*CUIDICH 'N RIGH*' (Help the King). The badge is in white metal.

Badge backing. A patch of Mackenzie tartan was worn behind the badge.

The Seaforth Highlanders was formed in 1881 from the 72nd and 78th Highlanders, both of which regiments had originally been raised by the Mackenzies of Seaforth. Although the 78th was obviously the junior of the two regiments, it was that regiment's cap-badge, the stag's head, which was adopted as the cap-badge of the new regiment, presumably because it was the badge of the Mackenzie Clan. The 72nd had the main device of its badge, an elephant, relegated to the new regiment's collar-badge.

During the Second World War the regiment raised six battalions, in addition to the two Regular battalions, and all served in an infantry role.

With the exception of the 5th (Caithness and Sutherland) Battalion (*qv*), all wore the above badge.

The Seaforth Highlanders
5TH (CAITHNESS AND SUTHERLAND) BATTALION TA

A cat sitting on a scroll within a circle inscribed '*SANS PEUR*' (without fear). The badge is white metal.

Badge backing. A patch of Government tartan was worn behind the badge.

The 5th (Caithness and Sutherland) Battalion of the Seaforth Highlanders had its origins in the volunteer movement of the nineteenth century when a volunteer unit was raised by the Duke of Sutherland. Consequently, it was his crest, a Cat-a-Mountain, together with his motto, which became the badge of the unit. It subsequently became the 1st Sutherland Highland Rifle Volunteers, but on the formation of the Territorial Force in 1908, it became part of the Seaforth Highlanders as that regiment's 5th Battalion.

After the Great War, the 5th Battalion was amalgamated with the 4th and re-designated the 4/5th Battalion and, as such, went to France with the BEF in 1939.

In 1940, the two battalions separated and the 5th regained its former title and its individual badge.

THE GORDON HIGHLANDERS

A stag's head above a ducal coronet within a wreath of ivy. On the bottom of the wreath is a scroll inscribed '*BY DAND*' (Stand fast). The badge is in white metal.

Badge backing. The badge was backed by a square of Gordon tartan.

The main device of the badge, the stag's head, ducal coronet and motto, was taken from the crest of the Duke of Gordon who, as Marquess of Huntley, raised the 92nd Regiment in 1794.

The Gordon Highlanders raised ten battalions during the Second World War, but not all continued to wear the regimental cap-badge. Four transferred to other arms and although they continued to retain their regimental title, they all wore the badge appropriate to the receiving arm.

4th (City of Aberdeen) Battalion. In 1939, the 4th Battalion was converted to a machine-gun unit and, as such, saw action with the BEF in France and Belgium. After its return to the United Kingdom, it was transferred to the Royal Artillery as the 92nd (Gordon Highlanders) Anti-Tank Regiment RA and wore artillery badges.

5th (Buchan and Formartin) Battalion. After serving with the BEF in 1939–40, the 5th Battalion was merged with the 9th Battalion in 1941 to form the 116th Regiment (Gordon Highlanders) Royal Armoured Corps and adopted the badge of the RAC.

8th Battalion. The 8th Battalion was converted to artillery as the 100th (Gordon Highlanders) Anti-Tank Regiment RA and wore Royal Artillery badges.

The Gordon Highlanders
THE LONDON SCOTTISH

An Andrew's Cross upon which is superimposed the Lion of Scotland, the whole upon a circle inscribed '*STRIKE SURE*'. On the lowest portion of the circle is inscribed '*SOUTH AFRICA 1900-02*'. On top of the cross is a scroll inscribed '*LONDON*' and at the bottom another inscribed '*SCOTTISH*'. A wreath of thistles surrounds the whole. The badge is in white metal.

Badge backing. Unlike other Scottish regiments, the London Scottish did not wear a tartan patch behind the badge. Instead, a patch of un-patterned hodden-grey cloth was worn.

The London Scottish was raised as a Volunteer unit in 1859 from Scots living in London and first saw active service in the Second Boer War, hence the battle-honour on the badge. In 1908, the London Scottish became the 14th Battalion of the London Regiment, but on the disbanding of the latter in 1937, the unit became part of the corps of the Gordon Highlanders.

During the Second World War the London Scottish raised three battalions. The 1st and 2nd Battalions continued in an infantry role and wore the above badge, but the 3rd Battalion was converted to artillery as the 97th Anti-Aircraft Regiment RA and adopted Royal Artillery badges.

THE QUEEN'S OWN CAMERON HIGHLANDERS

St Andrew with Cross within a wreath of thistles; on the lower portion of the wreath a scroll inscribed '*CAMERON*'. The badge is white metal.

Badge backing. A patch of Cameron of Erracht tartan was worn behind the badge. This tartan was unique in that it was not based, as were other Scottish regiments' tartans, on the Government tartan, but was specifically designed for the regiment.

The regiment was raised in 1793 as the 79th Foot by Sir Alan Cameron, and the badge of St Andrew with Cross is taken, as in other Scottish regiments, from the Order of the Thistle.

During the Second World War, six battalions of the regiment were raised. All served in an infantry role and all wore the above badge.

In addition, two battalions of the Liverpool Scottish were raised. Although part of the corps of Queen's Own Cameron Highlanders, they wore their own tartan and badge.

The Cameron Highlanders had the distinction of being the last regiment to wear the kilt in battle – at Dunkirk in 1940.

The Queen's Own Cameron Highlanders
THE LIVERPOOL SCOTTISH

St Andrew with Cross within a wreath of thistles. On either side of the cross is a scroll, inscribed *'LIVERPOOL'* and *'SCOTTISH'* respectively. At the foot of the wreath is a further scroll inscribed *'CAMERON'*. The badge is in white metal.

Badge backing. The badge was backed by a square of Forbes tartan.

The unit was originally raised, at the tune of the Second South African War, from Scots living in Liverpool, and until 1937 it was part of the King's Liverpool Regiment. Under AO/189/37 the Liverpool Scottish was transferred to the corps of the Queen's Own Cameron Highlanders and adopted the above badge. However, the regiment continued to wear the Forbes tartan behind the cap-badge, a tartan which had originally been adopted in 1900 as a compliment to its first Commanding Officer, Colonel C. Forbes Bell.

In 1939, when war was imminent and the Territorial Army was doubled, the Liverpool Scottish expanded to two battalions.

The 1st Battalion remained in the United Kingdom as a training regiment throughout the war, while in November 1942, the 2nd Battalion was transferred to the Royal Artillery as the 89th Anti-Tank Regiment RA and subsequently adopted artillery insignia.

THE ROYAL ULSTER RIFLES

An Irish Harp surmounted by an Imperial Crown. Below the harp is a scroll inscribed '*QUIS SEPARABIT*' (who shall separate us?). The badge is in white metal.

Badge backing. The 2nd Battalion wore a rectangular green patch behind the badge.

The harp and crown in the badge are taken, as is the motto; from the Order of St Patrick.

The Royal Ulster Rifles traced its origins back to 1793 when both its 1st and 2nd Battalions (the 83rd and 86th Regiments of Foot) were raised during the French Revolutionary Wars. In 1881 both regiments were linked to form the Royal Irish Rifles, but in 1920, following the foundation of the Irish Free State, the regiment changed its title, although the badge remained the same.

During the Second World War, the Royal Ulster Rifles raised six battalions and all but one continued to wear the above badge.

The exception was the 8th Battalion, which transferred to artillery as the 177th Light Anti-Aircraft Regiment RA. Although it adopted a Royal Artillery cap-badge, it was allowed to retain black RUR buttons on its uniform.

The Royal Ulster Rifles
THE LONDON IRISH RIFLES

The Irish Harp surmounted by an Imperial Crown. The badge is in blackened brass.

Unlike other Irish regiments, which have a harp as part of their badges, the London Irish Rifles has the original Irish Harp without the Maid of Erin.

Raised in 1859 as a Rifle Volunteer regiment from Irishmen living in London, the London Irish Rifles became part of the London Regiment on its formation in 1908. As its 18th Battalion it saw service in the Great War, becoming the 18th London Regiment (London Irish Rifles) in 1922.

On the disbandment of the London Regiment in 1937, the London Irish Rifles was transferred to the corps of the Royal Ulster Rifles. Despite these changes of title the above badge was retained.

During the Second World War, the London Irish Rifles raised two battalions, both of which wore the above badge.

THE ROYAL IRISH FUSILIERS (PRINCESS VICTORIA'S)

The cap-badge consists of two separate elements, one above the other. The top badge is the coronet of Queen Victoria, when Princess Victoria, and the lower badge is the ball of a grenade on which is an Irish Harp with the Prince of Wales's plume, coronet and motto. The coronet, together with the harp and the Prince of Wales's insignia on the grenade, are in white metal while the grenade itself is in gilding metal.

Badge backing. An inverted triangle of light green was worn behind the badge. This backing was originally worn by the regiment in the First World War when it served in 107th Brigade of the ill-fated 36th (Ulster) Division and was re-introduced until September 1943 when the 1st Battalion was serving in Italy – the original cloth being taken from the billiard table of the castle which was being used as the regimental headquarters.

The twin badges were drawn from the two regiments which, in 1881, amalgamated to form the Royal Irish Fusiliers. The grenade, with its embellishments, was taken from the 87th Foot, which having been raised as the Prince of Wales's Irish Regiment in 1793, became fusiliers in 1837. The 86th Foot, which became the 2nd Battalion of the new regiment, contributed the coronet having been, belatedly, granted the secondary title of ,Princess Victoria's, in 1866.

The above title of the regiment was, however, not adopted until after the First World War.

Four battalions of the regiment served in the Second World War and all wore the above badge.

THE ARGYLL AND SUTHERLAND HIGHLANDERS (PRINCESS LOUISE'S)

A circlet inscribed '*ARGYLL AND SUTHERLAND HIGHLANDERS*'. Within the circlet the cypher '*L*' of the late Princess Louise, interlaced, reversed and voided. On the left of the cypher is a boar's head and on the right, a cat. Above the cypher and resting upon the top part of the circlet is the Princess's coronet and the whole is within a wreath of thistles. The badge is in white metal.

Badge backing. The badge was backed by a square of Government tartan.

The badge drew its main devices from the cypher and coronet of Princess Louise, one of the daughters of Queen Victoria. Other features in the badge included the boar's head, which is the badge of the Argyll family, and the cat-a-mountain, which is that of the Sutherland family.

The regiment was formed in 1881 from the 91st (Princess Louise's Argyllshire) Highlanders and the 93rd Highlanders. However, the above title was only adopted in 1921.

Ten battalions served in the Second World War, but three, the 5th, 6th and 9th, transferred to the Royal Artillery and wore artillery insignia.

THE RIFLE BRIGADE (PRINCE CONSORT'S OWN)

A cross, as in the Order of the Bath, thereon a circlet inscribed '*THE RIFLE BRIGADE*' enclosing a bugle surmounted by a crown. The cross is enclosed within a wreath of laurel which has twined round it a number of scrolls inscribed with battle-honours. Battle-honours are also inscribed on each arm of the cross. Above the top arm of the cross and connecting the upper ends of the wreath is a tablet inscribed '*WATERLOO*' and surmounted by an Imperial Crown. On the lower portion of the wreath is a further scroll inscribed '*PRINCE CONSORT'S OWN*'. The badge is in white metal.

Badge backing. A backing of 'Rifle' green was adopted by some battalions, the shape of the backing depending upon the battalion.

The bugle in the centre of the badge was common to most Rifle regiments and, as these regiments did not carry colours, battle-honours were recorded on their badges. The major honour 'Waterloo' was granted to the regiment in 1815.

   The Rifle Brigade was formed as a Corps of Riflemen in 1800 and numbered as the 95th Foot. However, it was taken out of the numbered regiments of the line and designated the Rifle Brigade in 1816. The secondary title of 'Prince Consort's Own' was granted to the regiment in 1862 to commemorate the fact that the Prince Consort had been its Colonel-in-Chief for nine years until his death in 1861.

   When the London Regiment was disbanded in 1937, three of its battalions were transferred to the Rifle Brigade and became the Territorial component of the regiment. Two of these units continued their association with the Rifle Brigade

214

throughout the Second World War and were formally integrated into its battalion numbering in 1941.

The third unit, the Artists' Rifles, was converted to an Officer Cadet Training Unit in 1939 and, as such, ceased to have any connection with the Rifle Brigade.

The other two, the London Rifle Brigade and the Tower Hamlets Rifles, each expanded to two battalions on the doubling up of the Territorial Army in 1938, so that the Rifle Brigade entered the Second World War with six battalions, of which only the two Regular battalions wore the above badge. However, in 1941, the Territorial battalions were brought into the numbering of the Rifle Brigade and adopted the above badge.

Battalions of the regiment served in most major theatres of war; at one time no fewer than five were serving simultaneously in the Western Desert.

The Rifle Brigade (Prince Consort's Own)
THE LONDON RIFLE BRIGADE

The Royal Arms on a shield within a circlet inscribed on the upper portion '*LONDON RIFLE BRIGADE*' and on the lower portion with the battle-honour '*SOUTH AFRICA 1900–02*'. Immediately above the circlet a scroll inscribed with the battle-honour '*FRANCE AND FLANDERS 1914–18*' and, immediately below the circlet, another scroll inscribed '*YPRES 1915–17*'. Behind the circlet and shield are the crossed Sword and Mace of the City of London, enclosed in an oak leaf wreath which bears scrolls inscribed with four further battle-honours on each side. Below the Ypres scroll is another scroll inscribed '*PRIMUS IN URBS*' (First in the City) and below this again is an escutcheon of the Arms of the City of London (i.e. a shield bearing a cross, in the first quarter of which is a sword erect with its point upwards). The whole is surmounted by an Imperial Crown. The badge is in white metal.

The badge of the London Rifle Brigade was surely one of the most complicated ever worn, the various devices on it recording its somewhat complex derivation. The Royal Arms allude to HRH The Duke of Cambridge who was Honorary Colonel of the Regiment for over forty years from 1860 to 1904. The motto of the regiment refers to the fact that it was the first unit to be raised in the City of London during the threatened invasion by Napoleon III in 1859. In addition, the Sword, Mace and Arms of London represented on the badge were further evidence of the regiment's links with the City.

In common with other Rifle regiments, the London Rifle Brigade did not carry colours but displayed some of its major battle-honours on its badge.

The London Rifle Brigade was raised in 1859 as a unit of Rifle Volunteers but first saw active service in the Second Boer War, which accounted for its first battle-honour. On the formation of the London Regiment in 1908 it became the 5th (City of London) Battalion of that regiment and fought with distinction on the Western Front during the First World War. Following the disbandment of the London Regiment in 1937, the London Rifle Brigade was transferred to the corps of the Rifle Brigade when the above badge was adopted.

The London Rifle Brigade entered the Second World War with two battalions which, in 1941, were formally incorporated into the battalion numbering of the Rifle Brigade as its 7th and 8th Battalions. On doing so they ceased to wear the above badge.

The Rifle Brigade (Prince Consort's Own)
TOWER HAMLETS RIFLES

A cross based on the Order of the Bath and on the arms of which battle-honours are inscribed. In the centre of the cross, a circlet inscribed '*TOWER HAMLETS RIFLES – THE RIFLE BRIGADE*'. Within the circlet is a strung bugle surmounted by a crown. The whole is surrounded by a laurel wreath bearing scrolls inscribed with battle-honours. Above the cross and joining the ends of the laurel wreath is a tablet inscribed '*SOUTH AFRICA 1900–02*' and surmounted by an Imperial Crown. Across the base of the wreath is a scroll inscribed '*PRINCE CONSORT'S OWN*'. The badge is in white metal.

Originally the 26th Middlesex Rifle Volunteers, the regiment joined the London Regiment in 1908 as the 17th (County of London) Battalion (Poplar and Stepney Rifles). On the disbandment of the London Regiment in 1937 the battalion's title was changed to that shown above when the unit was incorporated into the Rifle Brigade. At the same time, the above badge was adopted. The badge was very closely modelled on that of the Rifle Brigade, even down to the positioning of the regiment's first battle-honour and the scroll inscribed 'Prince Consort's Own'.

Following the expansion of the Territorial Army in 1938, Tower Hamlets Rifles entered the Second World War with two battalions, but in 1940 a third battalion was raised. While the 1st and 2nd Battalions remained as part of the Rifle Brigade, in 1941 the 3rd Battalion was transferred to the Reconnaissance Corps as that formation's 5th Regiment. On its transfer, it adopted the badge and other insignia of the Reconnaissance Corps.

However, in 1941, the 1st and 2nd Battalions of the Tower Hamlets Rifles were formally incorporated into the Rifle Brigade as its 9th and 10th Battalions and ceased to wear the above badge.

218

SECTION VII

TERRITORIAL AND NON-REGULAR UNITS

THE RECONNAISSANCE CORPS

A vertical spear, point uppermost, and on each side, forked lightning meeting at the point of the spear. On the bottom of the spear and lightning is a scroll inscribed '*RECONNAISSANCE CORPS*'. The badge may be found in either white or gilding metal.

Badge backing. Apart from the 15th (Scottish) Regiment, which wore a green rectangular patch behind its badge, no backing was worn behind the badge.

The Reconnaissance Corps was formed in January 1941 from a number of independent Reconnaissance Squadrons and Anti-Tank Companies whose main purpose had been to provide intelligence to the infantry formations to which they had been attached. This function was formalised on the Corps' formation and no fewer than twenty-six regiments of the Corps were raised, many of them from the Territorial and war-service battalions of the infantry regiments which they served. However, two further regiments, the 81st and 82nd, were raised in West Africa and saw service in the Burma Campaign.

All regiments of the Corps wore the above badge with the exception of the 2nd Derbyshire Yeomanry, which continued to wear its own badge, and the 49th (West Riding) Regiment (*qv*).

In January 1944, in line with the increasing mechanisation of the Army, the Corps was transferred to the Royal Armoured Corps. Although it continued to wear its own badge, the Reconnaissance Corps adopted the black beret of the RAC.

THE RECONNAISSANCE CORPS
49TH (West Riding) Regiment

A vertical spear, point uppermost, with a white rose superimposed on the centre of the staff. On each side of the spear, forked lightning meeting at the head of the spear. Below the spear and the shafts of lightning, a scroll inscribed 'RECONNAISSANCE CORPS'. The badge is in white metal.

The 49th Regiment was formed in late 1942 from the 29th and 148th Independent Squadrons serving with the 49th (West Riding) Division. After spending the early years of its existence with the 49th Division in Iceland, the regiment was brought back to the United Kingdom to prepare for the Normandy landings. The regiment landed in France shortly after D-Day and subsequently fought throughout the North West Europe Campaign, ending the war in Northern Germany.

Towards the end of the war, the 49th Regiment added the White Rose of York as an unofficial embellishment on the centre of the spear on its badge. The badge was probably manufactured locally, with the rose originally being brazed onto a regular Reconnaissance Corps badge. However, while the badge of the parent corps is found in both gilding and white metal, that of the 49th Regiment occurs only in the latter.

THE HONOURABLE ARTILLERY COMPANY
(Infantry Battalion)

A fused grenade with the monogram '*HAC*' on the ball. The badge is in gilding metal.

The Honourable Artillery Company was granted a Charter of Incorporation in 1537 by King Henry VIII and, therefore, has probably a longer continuous history than any other military unit in the British Army. In 1871, it was organised into two branches, artillery and infantry, and the above badge was adopted by the latter.

In 1908 the Honourable Artillery Company was incorporated into the newly-formed London Regiment. However, unlike other Territorial units in London, the HAC did not take kindly to being incorporated into the London Regiment, and the Order, designating it as the 26th Battalion of that regiment, was soon rescinded.

Although it saw active service in the Great War, with two battalions serving in France, it was given a much different function in the Second World War. In 1939, the HAC infantry battalion became 162 (HAC) Officer Cadet Training Unit – a role it retained until November 1942. It was then absorbed into the Royal Armoured Corps OCTU at Sandhurst and ceased to wear the above badge.

THE ARTISTS' RIFLES

The heads of Mars and Minerva above a scroll inscribed 'ARTISTS'. The badge is in white metal.

The heads of Mars and Minerva represent war and the arts respectively and reflect the origins and composition of the regiment. The design of the badge was changed slightly in 1938, after the regiment left the London Regiment, when the inscription on the scroll was altered from 'Artists' Rifles' to that shown above.

Like many other Territorial regiments in London, the Artists' Rifles was originally raised in 1859 as a Rifle Volunteer unit. In 1881 it was attached to the Rifle Brigade but in 1908 was grouped with other volunteer units into the London Regiment, becoming the latter's 28th Battalion.

On the disbandment of the London Regiment the Artists' Rifles returned briefly to the corps of the Rifle Brigade. However, in 1939 it became 163 Officer Cadet Training Unit and ceased to have any further connection with the Rifle Brigade. Nevertheless, it continued to wear the above badge.

THE LOVAT SCOUTS

Within a strap inscribed '*JE SUIS PRET*' (I am ready), a stag's head on a torque. The badge is in white metal.

The badge, worn on a blue-diced bonnet, was the crest of the Frasers of Lovat and recalls the fact that the regiment was originally raised by Simon, 16th Lord Lovat, in 1900 for service in the Second Boer War.

In 1936, the Lovat Scouts, previously a Highland Yeomanry regiment, was given a new status as 'Mounted Scouts', which took precedence immediately after the Household Cavalry. The Lovat Scouts entered the Second World War in that role, being first part of the 9th (Scottish) Division and, subsequently, in early 1940, joining the Mounted Cavalry Division in England. However, following the German attack on Norway, it was dismounted and sent to guard the Faroe Islands against the threat of invasion. The regiment remained there in an infantry role until 1942.

Returning to Scotland in that year, the Lovat Scouts was formally transferred to the infantry, becoming the Mountain Reconnaissance Regiment of the 52nd (Lowland) Division. After ski-mountaineer training in the Canadian Rockies, the regiment was posted to Italy where it took part in the campaign until the end of the war.

THE HIGHLAND REGIMENT

A cross resembling St Andrew's Cross, but sharpened at each end; on the cross, a circular strap with the buckle on the left side, level with the centre of the cross. On the opposite side of the cross, a thistle; on the arms of the cross and within the circumference of the strap, two claymores, points uppermost. In the centre of the cross, a shield. At the top of the strap, the word '*HIGHLAND*' and at the bottom, the word '*REGIMENT*'. The badge is in white metal.

The Highland Regiment was raised in February 1942 and two battalions were formed. The 1st Battalion was drawn from the 70th Battalion, The Black Watch, while the 2nd Battalion had formerly been the 70th Battalion, The Argyll and Sutherland Highlanders.

The personnel of these two battalions consisted entirely of young soldiers and never at any time was it possible to enlist in the Highland Regiment or its lowland counterpart.

The Highland Regiment was disbanded under ACI 1563 of 1943; the 1st Battalion in August of that year and the 2nd Battalion on 1st January 1944, their personnel being transferred to other regiments or to the General Service Corps.

THE LOWLAND REGIMENT

St Andrew's Cross, thereon a thistle; below the thistle and twined round the lower portion of the cross, a scroll in two parts, the upper part inscribed '*LOWLAND*' and the lower inscribed '*REGIMENT*'. The badge is in white metal.

The Lowland Regiment, like the Highland Regiment, was formed in February 1942.

The regiment was made up of young soldiers drawn largely from the 70th Battalion of The Royal Scots. Unlike its highland counterpart, the Lowland Regiment never expanded to more than one battalion and during its relatively brief existence the regiment remained virtually what the 70th Battalion had been, namely, a training regiment.

The Lowland Regiment was disbanded in 1943 and its members dispersed to other regiments and the General Service Corps.

SECTION VIII

CORPS OF THE SERVICES

THE ROYAL ARMY SERVICE CORPS

An eight-pointed star, the top-most point being replaced by an Imperial Crown resting on the Garter and in a voided centre, the Royal Cypher. Below the Garter a scroll inscribed '*ROYAL ARMY SERVICE CORPS*' with laurel sprays emanating from each end of the scroll to meet the crown. The badge is in gilding metal.

The Royal Army Service Corps traced its origins back to 1794, when a Corps of Wagoners was formed to meet the demands of the British Army in its European campaigns during the Napoleonic Wars. The Corps did not survive the end of those wars, but was revised in the form of the Land Transport Corps in the Crimean War.

It became the Army Service Corps in 1870 but split into two divisions when the Army Ordnance Corps was established in 1875. In 1881 the Army Ordnance Corps became a corps in its own right and the title of the remaining division, responsible for the issuing and provisioning of food and for the transport function of the Army, was changed to the Commissariat and Transport Corps. The title was only in use for seven years, after which the previous designation of the Army Service Corps was resumed. At the same time, the forerunner of the above badge was adopted. However, the above badge was not introduced until 1918 when the Corps was granted the prefix 'Royal' in recognition of its services in the Great War.

In the Second World War the RASC's responsibilities expanded almost exponentially because of the global nature of the conflict and the greater need for transport. As a result, by the end of the war over 10 per cent of all British Army personnel were serving in the corps.

THE ROYAL ARMY MEDICAL CORPS

The rod of Aesculapius with a serpent twined round it within a scroll of laurel. The whole is ensigned by an Imperial Crown. Below is a scroll inscribed 'ROYAL ARMY MEDICAL CORPS'. The badge is in gilding metal.

The main device of the badge, the rod entwined with a serpent, is taken from Greek mythology being the symbol of Aesculapius, the Greek god of Medicine.

Like many functions in the British Army, the care of the sick and wounded was initially a regimental responsibility. It was not until the horrors of the Crimean War were recognised that the Army Hospital Corps was formed in 1857, composed largely of male nurses and orderlies. This, in turn, became the Medical Staff Corps in 1884.

Meanwhile, in 1873 medical officers had been formed into a corps and the two formations were eventually amalgamated into the Royal Army Medical Corps in 1898. The corps adopted the rod of Aesculapius as the main device for its badge and the current design dates from 1902 when the Imperial Crown replaced the Victorian crown on the laurel wreath.

Although a non-combatant corps, the RAMC suffered heavy casualties during the Second World War and had the distinction of having two members win the Victoria Cross.

THE ROYAL ARMY ORDNANCE CORPS

The Garter bearing its motto surmounted by an Imperial Crown. Within the Garter a shield bearing the Arms of the Board of Ordnance. Below the Garter is a scroll inscribed '*ROYAL ARMY ORDNANCE CORPS*'. The badge is in gilding metal.

The Royal Army Ordnance Corps was responsible for the provisioning and issuing of all munitions and equipment to the Army and traced its origins back to the Board of Ordnance in the sixteenth century. It is from that Board that the shield in the centre of the badge was taken and reflected the historical continuity of the function, if not the name, of the corps.

With the abolition of the Board of Ordnance in the nineteenth century, responsibility for its function was passed to the War Office Stores Branch, which, in 1875, became a separate division of the Army Service Corps. In 1881 an Army Ordnance Corps was established as a corps in its own right, but this was an Other Ranks' corps only, officers being found from the Army Ordnance Department. It was not until 1918 that the two formations were amalgamated and given the prefix 'Royal' for services in the Great War. The above badge dates from the amalgamation.

As the corps had responsibility for the provision of all equipment which the Army used, it was present in every major campaign of the 1939–45 war, almost 5 per cent of the total Army strength wearing the RAOC badge.

THE ROYAL MECHANICAL AND ELECTRICAL ENGINEERS

Four shields, each bearing one of the initials of the corps title, placed upon a laurel wreath in the form of a cross, with a pair of calipers in the centre. The whole is ensigned with an Imperial Crown. The badge is in gilding metal.

The calipers on the badge were a symbolic representation of the engineering function of the corps.

The significant developments which occurred in the Army's mechanical and electrical equipment in the early years of the Second World War indicated a need for the concentration of expertise in one corps. To this end, the Royal Mechanical and Electrical Engineers was formed in October 1942. Its personnel were drawn from technicians in the Royal Engineers, the Royal Army Service Corps and the Royal Army Ordnance Corps and the corps was tasked with the repair and maintenance of nearly every piece of Army equipment, from armoured vehicles to radar.

As might be expected, the corps served in almost every theatre of war, playing a particularly important role in those areas like the Western Desert and North West Europe where armour was the decisive weapon.

THE CORPS OF MILITARY POLICE

The Royal Cypher surmounted by an Imperial Crown within a laurel wreath. Below the wreath is a scroll inscribed '*MILITARY POLICE*'. The badge is in gilding metal.

Badge backing. Although not officially sanctioned, a red insert was often worn behind the badge.

The corps was only established as a regular corps of the British Army in 1855 when a number of NCOs were formed into a corps to undertake duties which had previously been a regimental responsibility. In 1885 the corps was divided into the Military Mounter Police and the Military Foot Police. The two corps were re-united in 1926 and given the above title, the badge being closely modelled on that of the Military Mounted Police.

THE ROYAL ARMY PAY CORPS

The Royal Crest with an Imperial Crown over a scroll inscribed '*FIDE ET FIDUCIA*' (in faith and trust). The Royal Crest is in gilding metal and the scroll is in white metal.

Although the Royal Army Pay Corps only dates from 1920, its two antecedents – the Army Pay Department and the Army Pay Corps – were formed in the latter half of the nineteenth century. The original badge of the Royal Army Pay Corps consisted simply of a monogram RAPC surmounted by the Royal Crest, but in 1929, in recognition of the outstanding services performed by the corps in the Great War, King George V approved the grant of the motto '*Fide et Fiducia*'. At the same time, the corps' badge was re-designed and the RAPC monogram was dispensed with. Instead, the Royal Crest over the new motto was adopted.

The RAPC saw service in every theatre of war, including airborne operations at Arnhem.

THE ROYAL ARMY VETERINARY CORPS

A centaur within a laurel wreath and ensigned with an Imperial Crown. Below the wreath is a scroll inscribed *'ROYAL ARMY VETERINARY CORPS'*. The badge is in gilding metal.

The centaur of Greek mythology was chosen as the badge of the Royal Army Veterinary Corps to reflect the role of the corps in which man combined with the horse to serve the needs of the Army.

Although there had been an Army Veterinary Service established as early as 1796, regiments were still responsible for the veterinary services which were provided for their horses. It was not until 1881 that the Army Veterinary Department was formed and took over from the existing regimental system. However, this was an all-officer formation, the other ranks still being drawn from the regiments in which they served. In 1903 the Army Veterinary Corps was formed with the primary role of attending to the horses, not only of the cavalry, but of the artillery and other arms and corps. Its composition was initially restricted to SNCOs and men, but in 1906 the Army Veterinary Department and the Army Veterinary Corps were combined into the AVC.

In recognition of its services in the Great War, the corps was awarded the prefix Royal in 1918 when the above badge was adopted. Although with the mechanisation of the cavalry and artillery, the horse virtually disappeared from service in the Army, the RAVC played an important role in the Second World War tending to other animals – mules and dogs, for example – which were still needed in certain theatres of war.

THE SMALL ARMS SCHOOL CORPS

A Vickers machine-gun and thereon a pair of crossed rifles with bayonets fixed, with an Imperial Crown within the angle formed by the rifles above the machine-gun. The whole is within a laurel wreath and on the wreath are scrolls inscribed: on the left side 'SMALL', on the bottom 'ARMS' and on the right 'SCHOOL'. The badge is in gilding metal.

The rifles and the machine-gun depicted on the badge reflected the origins and the functions of the corps.

The Small Arms School Corps originated in the School of Musketry which was formed in 1855, which became, in 1919, the Small Arms School, Hythe. In 1926 a Machine Gun School was established at Netheravon and these two schools were combined into the Small Arms School Corps three years later. The badge dates from this amalgamation.

The purpose of the school was to train regimental instructors and others who had a need to have special expertise in the use of small arms.

THE MILITARY PROVOST STAFF CORPS

The Royal Cypher surmounted by an Imperial Crown. The badge is in gilding metal.

The Military Prison Staff Corps was formed in 1901 and was re-designated as the Military Provost Staff Corps in 1906. On its formation the corps adopted the Royal Cypher as its badge, but during the reign of King George V, the cypher was surrounded by a laurel wreath. On the accession of King George VI, the MPSC reverted to using the Royal Cypher without the adornment of a wreath.

The Military Provost Staff Corps consisted of Senior NCOs recruited from other regiments and corps, their function being to form the staffs of Military Prisons, detention barracks etc.

THE ARMY EDUCATIONAL CORPS

An open book superimposed on crossed lances and rifles, the pennons of the lances facing outwards. Below the butts of the rifles and lances is a scroll inscribed '*ARMY EDUCATIONAL CORPS*'. The badge is in gilding metal.

The Army Educational Corps traced its origins to the Corps of Army Schoolmasters which was formed in the nineteenth century to ensure basic standards of literacy and numeracy among new recruits in the Army.

The rapid increase in the size of the Army during the First World War demonstrated the need for a more comprehensive educational programme. As a result, the Army Educational Corps was established in 1920 and the above badge, symbolising military education, was introduced at the same time. The AEC not only subsumed the role of the Corps of Army Schoolmasters, but was given a much wider remit in the field of army education.

THE ARMY DENTAL CORPS

A laurel wreath surmounted by an Imperial Crown. Within the wreath is the monogram '*ADC*'. The badge is in gilding metal.

The first dentist to serve with the Army was a member of the staff of Guy's Hospital Dental School who went to South Africa at his own expense during the Second Boer War. Although a further four dental surgeons were sent out in the later stages of that war, there was a general indifference in the Army to the dental health of its personnel, even though no fewer than 2000 men were evacuated back to the United Kingdom on purely dental grounds.

The indifference continued into the First World War, but eventually a number of dental surgeons were recruited and attached to the Royal Army Medical Corps. The Army Dental Corps was formed in January 1921 and was able to provide a comprehensive scheme of dental treatment for personnel in both the Army and the Royal Air Force. It was not until 1930 that an RAF Dental Branch was formed to take responsibility for air force personnel.

Dental surgeons served on all fronts in the Second World War, both in hospitals and with mobile field ambulances. In addition to attending to normal dental problems, invaluable service was rendered by the ADC in the treatment of jaw injuries and facial disfigurement received by personnel in action.

THE PIONEER CORPS

A pile, consisting of a pick, head downwards, placed centrally, with a rifle crossing in front of it from the left and a shovel crossing between the rifle and the pick from the right. On the pile, a laurel wreath with the branches pointing downwards; the whole ensigned by an Imperial Crown. Below the pile a scroll inscribed '*LABOR OMNIA VINCIT*' (Labour conquers all things). The badge is in gilding metal.

The three implements depicted in the badge represented the function of the corps and confirmed its combatant status.

The Pioneer Corps traced its origins to the Labour Corps of the First World War. In 1939, the Labour Companies of the Royal Engineers were formed into the Auxiliary Military Pioneer Corps, but in July 1940, under Army Order 200/40, the title was changed to the Pioneer Corps.

The change in title also reflected a fundamental change in status, for unlike the Labour Companies, the Pioneer Corps was fully combatant and personnel in the corps served in every major theatre of war. By 1945 it was one of the numerically largest formations in the Army with over 275,000 men in its ranks.

THE INTELLIGENCE CORPS

A rose within two branches of laurel and ensigned with an Imperial Crown. Below the laurel is a scroll inscribed '*INTELLIGENCE CORPS*'. The badge is in gilding metal.

The rose, the emblem of secrecy, was the main device of the Intelligence Corps. The corps was raised in July 1940 following the increasing demands which had been placed on military intelligence by the British Expeditionary Force during its campaign in France and Belgium in 1939–40. Prior to its establishment, intelligence had been carried out by officers and men seconded from regimental duties.

THE ARMY PHYSICAL TRAINING CORPS

Crossed swords surmounted by an Imperial Crown. The badge is in either white or gilding metal.

The Army Gymnastic Staff, as it was first designated, was formed in 1860 and became the Army Physical Training Corps in September 1940. However, the above badge pre-dated the formation of the corps, being introduced in 1902.

The expansion of the British Army in 1939–40 and the poor physical standards of many of the recruits substantially increased the demands on the Army physical training staff. As a result, the new corps was formed not only to incorporate Army PT staff but to implement and administer Army physical training policy.

THE ARMY CATERING CORPS

An ancient Grecian brazier within a circlet inscribed '*ARMY CATERING CORPS*' ensigned with an Imperial Crown. The badge is in gilding metal.

The main device of the badge is a Grecian brazier to symbolise cooking.

The Army Catering Corps was formed in March 1941 to meet the complex demands of feeding the more mobile armies in the Second World War. Until then, cooking had been a regimental responsibility, but with the advent of the ACC, the whole range of functions associated with the feeding of war-time armies, from provisioning to the training of catering personnel, was brought under the control of a single corps.

THE GENERAL SERVICE CORPS

Two badges were worn:

left. The Royal Arms

right. The Royal Crest, a lion on an Imperial Crown, superimposed upon crossed swords. Below the Royal Crest, a scroll inscribed '*DEUS VULT*' (It is God's will). Below the scroll is a decorative motif incorporating the rose, thistle, leek and shamrock.

Both badges are in gilding metal.

The General Service Corps was formed in February 1942 to provide a 'pool' into which recruits were placed when first joining the Army to determine the most suitable arm or corps in which they should serve. During this period of their service they wore the first of the two badges.

In 1944 the second badge, composed of the British Army badge and a representation of the national plants of the United Kingdom, was introduced. It was worn by permanent staff in the training battalions of the General Service Corps and represented the service of the corps given to the whole of the Army.

THE AUXILIARY TERRITORIAL SERVICE

The initials '*ATS*' within a laurel wreath surmounted by an Imperial Crown. The badge is in gilding metal.

The Auxiliary Territorial Service was formed in September 1938 as the counterpart to the Women's Auxiliary Army Corps of the First World War. Initially its members were enrolled, not enlisted, and its officers were not commissioned. ATS personnel were not accorded full military status until 1941 and yet, at its peak, the strength of the corps was almost 250,000, serving in areas as diverse as the Middle East, North West Europe, the West Indies and Africa.

WOMEN'S TRANSPORT SERVICE (F.A.N.Y.)

A circlet inscribed 'WOMEN'S TRANSPORT SERVICE F.A.N.Y.' with, in the centre, a cross moline. The badge is in bronze.

Originally formed in 1907 as a corps of horsewomen trained in first aid, the First Aid Nursing Yeomanry was mechanised by 1914 and served in ambulance units on the Western Front in the Great War. In 1933, its name was changed to the Women's Transport Service and the above badge adopted.

The Women's Transport Service continued to provide drivers for the Army throughout the Second World War.

SECTION IX

BADGE BACKINGS AND INSERTS

Badge backings and inserts of those regiments which adopted them during the Second World War are given below. While some regiments entered the war with backings to their badges, the majority of such embellishments were not worn until after the cap GS was introduced.

In the case of some infantry regiments, not all battalions necessarily wore the same backing. Where this is the case, the details of specific battalion backings are given in italics.

CAVALRY

4th/7th Royal Dragoon Guards	A maroon square worn on its point cut to the outer edges of the four main points of the star
5th Royal Inniskilling Dragoon Guards	A red outline
10th Royal Hussars (Prince of Wales's Own)	A domed red patch
15th/19th The King's Royal Hussars	A scarlet outline
22nd Dragoons	A green diamond (approx 2¼ inches by 1½ inches) the longer length being in the vertical
23rd Hussars	A dark green domed patch
26th Hussars	A diamond patch consisting of three vertical stripes: blue, yellow and maroon
The Royal Wiltshire Yeomanry (Prince of Wales's Own)	A rectangular scarlet patch (approx 1¾ inches high by 2½ inches)
The Yorkshire Hussars (Alexandra, Princess of Wales's Own)	A red outline

The Staffordshire Yeomanry (The Queen's Own Regiment)	A circular red patch (approx 1¼ inches in diameter)
1st Northamptonshire Yeomanry	A circular royal blue patch (approx 1¾ inches in diameter)
2nd Northamptonshire Yeomanry	A royal blue insert behind the voided centre of the badge

ARTILLERY

The Queen's Own Dorset Yeomanry	A rectangular patch of dark green (approx 2¼ inches by 2 inches)
The Berkshire Yeomanry	A black rectangle (approx 2⅜ inches by 1½ inches)
The Norfolk Yeomanry	A 2-inch yellow square
The Monmouthshire Regiment *1st Battalion*	*A 2-inch square of 'Rifle' green*

ARMY AIR CORPS

The Parachute Regiment *5th (Scottish) Battalion*	*A diamond of Hunting Stuart tartan (approx 2½ inches square)*

INFANTRY

The Royal Scots (The Royal Regiment)	A 3-inch square of Hunting Stuart tartan (all battalions)
1st and 3rd Battalions	*A red insert behind the voided centre of the badge*
2nd Battalion	*A green insert behind the voided centre of the badge*
The King's Own Royal Regiment (Lancaster)	A red rectangle (3 inches by 2 inches)
The Royal Northumberland Fusiliers	A 2-inch square of gosling green on which a red V was superimposed
The Royal Fusiliers (City of London Regiment)	A 2-inch square divided vertically into maroon and dark blue halves

The King's Regiment (Liverpool)	
2nd Battalion	*A red 1⅞ inch square*
8th Battalion	*A green outline*
The Royal Norfolk Regiment	
1st Battalion	*A black rectangle (2 inches by 2½ inches deep)*
The Suffolk Regiment	A red insert behind the voided centre of the badge
The Somerset Light Infantry (Prince Albert's)	A 2-inch square of Light Infantry green
The Green Howards (Alexandra, Princess of Wales's Own Yorkshire Regiment)	A 2-inch square of grass green
The Royal Scots Fusiliers	A 3-inch square of Government tartan
The King's Own Scottish Borderers	A 3-inch square of Lesley tartan
The Cameronians (Scottish Rifles)	A 3-inch square of Douglas tartan
The Royal Inniskilling Fusiliers	A red triangle (base 3½ inches by 1¾ inches)
The Worcestershire Regiment	A rectangle of emerald green (approx 2 inches high by 2 inches)
The Duke of Cornwall's Light Infantry	A red insert behind the voided centre of the badge. In addition, from 1943, a 2-inch patch of Light Infantry green was worn behind the badge
The Duke of Wellington's Regiment	A red triangle with rounded corners
The Border Regiment	A red insert behind the voided centre of the badge
The South Staffordshire Regiment	A light brown hessian patch (The Holland Patch)
The Dorsetshire Regiment	A 2-inch square of dark green
The South Lancashire Regiment (The Prince of Wales's Volunteers)	A red insert behind the voided centre of the badge

The Black Watch (The Royal Highland Regiment)	A 3-inch square of Government tartan
The Tyneside Scottish	A 3-inch square of Government tartan

Oxfordshire and Buckinghamshire
Light Infantry

2nd Battalion	*A circular patch of Light Infantry green (2 inches in diameter) when it became an airborne unit in 1941*
1st and 2nd Buckinghamshire Battalions	*A Rifle red outline*
The Essex Regiment	A patch of 'Pompadour' purple, the shape depending upon the battalion
1st Battalion	*A diamond shaped patch*
2nd Battalion	*A circular patch*

(*some of the war-service battalions wore no patch*)

The Sherwood Foresters (Nottinghamshire and Derbyshire Regiment)	A 2-inch square of Lincoln green (*except for the 6th Bn which wore the patch in the form of a diamond*)
The Northamptonshire Regiment	A black circular patch (1¾ inches in diameter)
The Royal Berkshire Regiment (Princess Charlotte of Wales's)	An inverted red triangle (approx 2 inches wide by 2½ inches deep)
The King's Own Yorkshire Light Infantry	A patch of Light Infantry green (2½ inches by 1½ inches deep)
The King's Shropshire Light Infantry	A patch of Light Infantry green, the shape depending upon the battalion
1st Battalion	*A green outline*
2nd Battalion	*A 2½-inch circular patch*
3rd Battalion	*A rectangular patch (2 inches by 2½ inches)*

The Herefordshire Regiment

1st Battalion	*A 2-inch square of green*
2nd Battalion	*A 2-inch square of red*

The King's Royal Rifle Corps	A Rifle red outline
The Wiltshire Regiment (The Duke of Edinburgh's) *2nd and 4th Battalions*	*A 2-inch maroon square*
5th Battalion	*A 2-inch blue square*
The Durham Light Infantry *1st Battalion*	*A 2-inch square of Light infantry green*

(with the exception of the 6th Battalion, most other battalions wore a circular green patch)

6th Battalion	*A 2-inch square of Rifle red*
The Highland Light Infantry (City of Glasgow Regiment)	A 3-inch square of Mackenzie tartan
The Glasgow Highlanders	A 3-inch square of Government tartan
The Seaforth Highlanders (The Ross-shire Buffs, The Duke of Albany's) tartan	A 3-inch square of Mackenzie
5th (Caithness and Sutherland) Battalion	*A 3-inch square of Government tartan*
The Gordon Highlanders	A 3-inch square of Gordon tartan
The London Scottish	A 3-inch square of unpatterned hodden-grey cloth
The Queen's Own Cameron Highlanders	A 3-inch square of Cameron of Erracht tartan
The Liverpool Scottish	A 3-inch square of Forbes tartan
The Royal Ulster Rifles *2nd Battalion*	*A rectangular green patch (2 inches wide by 2¼ inches high)*
The Royal Irish Fusiliers (Princess Victoria's)	An inverted triangle of light green (2 inches wide by 2½ inches deep)
The Argyll and Sutherland Highlanders (Princess Louise's)	A 3-inch square of Government tartan
The Rifle Brigade (Prince Consort's)	A backing of Rifle red, the shape depending upon the battalion
The Reconnaissance Corps *15th (Scottish) Regiment*	*A green rectangle (3 inches by 2 inches)*

Bibliography

Audax C.E.	*Badge Backings and Special Embellishments of the British Army*	UDR Benevolent Fund 1992
Bloomer W.H. & K.D.	*Scottish Regimental Badges 1793–1971*	Arms & Armour Press 1982
Davis B.L.	*British Army Uniforms and Insignia of World War Two*	Arms & Armour Press 1983
Edwards T.J.	*Regimental Badges* (First Edition)	Charles Knight 1972
Frederick J.B.M.	*Lineage Book of the British Land Forces*	Microfilms Academic 1978
Gaylor J.	*Military Badge Collecting*	Seeley Service 1973
Kipling A.L. & King H.L.	*Head-dress Badges of the British Army* (Volumes 1 and 2)	Muller 1979
Mileham P.J.R.	*The Yeomanry Regiments*	Spellmount 1985
Mollo B.	*The Sharpshooters*	Historical Research Unit 1971
Wilkinson F.	*Badges of the British Army 1820–1960*	Arms & Armour Press 1971

Regimental Index